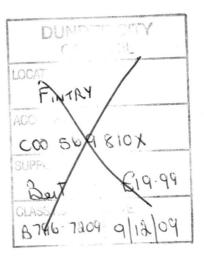

Jenson
Button

A WORLD CHAMPION'S STORY

Parts of this book were originally published in October 2004
as Jenson Button: The Unauthorised Biography
Published in November 2009

A catalogue record for this book is available from the British Library

ISBN 978 1 84425 936 6

Library of Congress catalog card no 2009933826

Published by Haynes Publishing,
Sparkford, Yeovil, Somerset BA22 7JJ, UK.
Tel: 01963 442030 Fax: 01963 440001
Int. tel: +44 1963 442030 Int. fax: +44 1963 440001
E-mail: sales@haynes.co.uk
Website: www.haynes.co.uk

Haynes North America Inc.,
861 Lawrence Drive, Newbury Park,
California 91320, USA.

Designed by Lee Parsons

Printed and bound in the UK

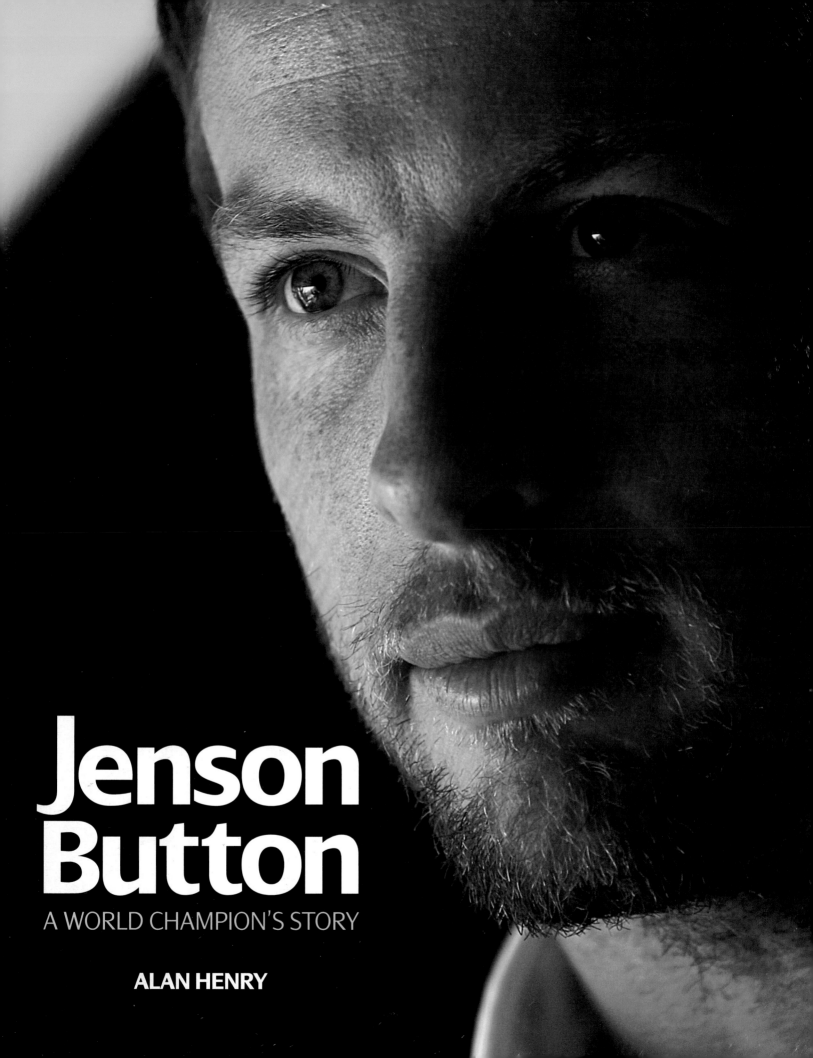

Jenson Button

A WORLD CHAMPION'S STORY

ALAN HENRY

CONTENTS

INTRODUCTION

For a guy who failed his driving test at his first attempt, it was pretty overwhelming stuff. In fact, by any standards, for Jenson Button it was a totally overwhelming occasion, the realisation of a lifetime's dream. Mark Webber was already well into his slowing-down lap, celebrating victory in the 2009 Brazilian Grand Prix at Interlagos, long before Jenson came into view up the long hill onto the startline straight at the legendary Sao Paulo circuit. But it was Jenson they were all waiting for.

Suddenly, the white and lime liveried Brawn-Mercedes burst into view. A couple of hundred yards more and the job was done. Fifth place was good enough. On his 169th outing behind the wheel of a Formula 1 car, the 29-year-old from Somerset had finally won the World Championship, crowning a year which had seen him win six of the season's first seven races, driving for a team which had looked as though it might not even exist only three weeks before the first race of the 2009 title campaign.

Thus the 10th British World Champion in 51 years was crowned in the down-at-heel, yet compellingly enthusiastic, chaos of the Interlagos paddock on a rain-threatening afternoon in October. Jenson was continuing a great tradition started in 1958 by the late Mike Hawthorn, a man who died 21 years before the 2009 World Drivers' Champion was born. It was a fine performance, topping off a brilliant job by everybody at the Brawn-Mercedes team, who rescued a mathematically wavering scenario

to help deliver to their boy the biggest prize on offer.

Button's story isn't quite rags to riches, but it's pretty close. With his father John's unwavering support, the fresh-faced youngster from Frome climbed through the cut-and-thrust of the teenage kart-racing scene to muscle his way into first Formula Ford, then F3. In 1998 he won the BRDC McLaren *Autosport* Young Driver of the Year award, and the £50,000 cheque that went with it was certainly a useful boost to his plans to move into F3 the following year. Part of that prize was also a test drive in an F1 McLaren-Mercedes, a treat which eventually took place almost a year later in dank and damp conditions at Silverstone.

By this time Button had finished third in the '99 British F3 Championship. He proved to be a natural and, at this early stage in his career, he was already being targeted as a possible F1 candidate for the following year. A test at the wheel of a Prost-Peugeot F1 car – generously offered with no strings attached – had shown Button to be startlingly composed in the sport's most senior category. The test took place at Barcelona's Circuit de Catalunya where, only five months earlier, Jenson had scrounged a paddock pass in order to gain access to F1's inner sanctum. Within another five months he would be a full-time member of that exclusive community.

Right from the start, there has been a lack of complication, but not of sophistication, about Jenson Button. The F1 road he has trodden towards the

World Championship has not always been simple or straightforward, but he has remained consistently good natured and well balanced in the face of the many ups and downs. His F1 career began on a promising note with Williams in 2000, only to seem as if it was likely to be sluiced into oblivion over the following two seasons by the joint efforts of Benetton and Renault, and their largely arthritic machinery.

Throughout the 2000 season, Jenson seemed in harmony with the Williams squad. Sadly, it was not going to last. Frank Williams had a residual obligation to Juan Pablo Montoya, the highly promising Colombian driver, for the 2001 season, and Button had entered into his contract with the team knowing full well that it might only last for a year. So it proved. Montoya duly joined the team as Ralf Schumacher's team-mate for 2001, and scored his maiden grand prix victory at Monza that year, five years before Jenson would do the same. Poignantly, by the time Button clinched the 2009 World Championship, Montoya had long departed from F1, having never quite delivered on that early promise. Such are the ironies of this complex sport.

For 2001, Jenson would come within the orbit of Flavio Briatore, the charismatic and controversial team principal of the Benetton-Renault team, which would be officially re-branded as the Renault works team in 2002. It was to prove a bruisingly disappointing season for the 21-year-old. A fifth place in the German Grand Prix

earned him his sole championship points of the season, and he finished the year 17th overall in the standings.

In 2002 things were significantly better. Jenson netted 14 points to take seventh place in the Drivers' Championship, but by the middle of the season he knew he would be moving on. Briatore had decided to promote the Renault team's test driver Fernando Alonso to take Jenson's place for 2003. So, the young Englishman accepted an offer from David Richards, the BAR-Honda team principal, to join his team for 2003.

At the age of 23, Jenson Button was now steering a path which, although somewhat convoluted, would eventually carry him to World Championship glory. Yet there were times when it really looked as though it would never happen. Winning his first Grand Prix was difficult enough, a task not achieved until Hungary in the summer of 2006. And it would take the best part of another three seasons before he would win his second – a dominant demonstration of driving prowess in Melbourne – to kick off a championship assault in which he was never headed in the points table, right up to the day on which he secured the crown.

The 2009 season was truly momentous. It had started with Ross Brawn, the former Honda F1 team principal, buying control of the team after the Japanese car maker decided that it would withdraw from F1 due to the global recession. Brawn and the team's CEO, Nick Fry, aided by a brilliantly dedicated workforce, laboured through the winter in the face of uncertainty to have a couple of Mercedes-engined cars on the grid for the first race in Melbourne. A stunning performance in pre-season testing had provided a warning to the established front-runners that the plain white and lime Brawn GP cars, devoid of sponsorship, meant business. Jenson and his team-mate, Rubens Barrichello, were up and running, albeit against the odds.

Button's victories came thick and fast. The Englishman's Brawn was first past the flag in Australia, Malaysia, Bahrain, Spain, Monaco and Turkey, building up a healthy points lead. This early-season performance would help insulate his advantage against marauding rivals – including Barrichello and Red Bull team-mates Sebastian Vettel and Mark Webber – during a relatively barren mid-season spell, where points, let alone wins, seemed hard to come by.

There were even those who felt that Jenson was perhaps losing his touch, or trying to race too tactically, or both. But that bold, title-clinching run from 14th on the grid to fifth at the chequered flag in Brazil reminded us all that there was fire in his belly, and his world class shone through strongly despite all his setbacks.

Jenson has successfully negotiated every pitfall and snag which has blocked his path over the years, however fleetingly, with grace and an attractively detached sense of dignity and humour. Never one to sulk or stamp his feet when things went wrong, it was heartening to see him give a huge bear-hug to his father John after he had achieved both their lifetimes' ambition when he crossed the finishing line at Interlagos.

So, Button proved he was a worthy and deserving World Champion. A decent man who had reached the summit of his own personal Everest. And he did it during the course of a Grand Prix highlighted by a succession of bold overtaking manoeuvres from the number 22 Brawn which were a delight to witness. It was a performance which bore the unalloyed stamp of a real racer.

As he dozed fitfully the next morning, at 35,000 feet over the Atlantic ocean, while his team-mate Rubens Barrichello's luxurious Embraer Legacy private jet whisked him at 500mph towards England, and the plaudits of his home fans, in every sense of the expression Jenson Button had arrived at the top of the world. In an F1 community which can be waspish and jealous in pretty much equal measure, his was a success which was universally applauded.

A lifetime's ambition realised. Jenson raises his hand to acknowledge the salutes of the Brawn team as he crosses the line at Interlagos in the Brazilian Grand Prix to become the 2009 World Champion.

sutton-images.com

[01]

ON THE LOWER RUNGS OF THE LADDER

Making it to the motor racing big time can be a frustrating and bruising experience for the ambitious young talent. There are signposts along the way indicating what is thought to be the best and most reasoned route to pursue, but they are not always obvious. Opportunities present themselves, but often prove to be shimmering illusions. Choices that appear to be the right ones to make in the middle of a season, when focusing on the following year, can turn out to be incorrect and ill-timed when the moment finally arrives to take them up.

We're talking about the 'what if' factor. What if Frank Williams had not been bound by a residual obligation to promote Juan Pablo Montoya to his F1 team in 2001? Had Button been able to stay after his freshman year in 2000, would he have won the three Grand Prix victories which fell to Ralf Schumacher, and the one win which fell to Montoya?

Similarly, had Flavio Briatore opted to keep Button in 2003 rather than promoting Fernando Alonso from the role of test driver, would Jenson have been in with a chance of winning the 2005 and 06 World Championships?

Moreover, to spin the roulette wheel in a negative direction, would Button have sunk without trace if he had taken the decision to move to Renault in 2009, a switch which he hinted had been on the cards during the period when Honda was vacillating over whether or not to stay in F1. As Jenson remarked with some irony, Briatore may have

likened him to a 'concrete post' in an off-the-cuff comment early in 2009, so why had he spent so much time trying to persuade that so-called concrete post to drive for him that season?

Or how would it have been if Peter Sauber had successfully concluded negotiations to tempt Button to join his Swiss-based team in 2003? Would he have enjoyed better times with the team which was eventually transformed into the BMW-Sauber squad? Or would he have faltered and dropped from view?

Of course, this is all running ahead of events for the young man who grew up in modest circumstances in Frome, a medium sized town in rural Somerset where there has always been a definite sense of pride and protection towards the privacy of their most recent celebrity inhabitant. When some of Jenson Button's friends began to suspect that a national newspaper might be snooping around, trying to tempt them into dishing the dirt on the now-famous Formula 1 driver, there was an almost public plea for everybody to protect their man from what they clearly regarded as an unwarranted intrusion.

Pupils at Selwood Middle School had been approached discreetly, as were two members of Jenson's year group at Frome Community College. It sounds as though these prying members of the media were given short shrift. "I know that the whole of Frome is so pleased and proud of Jenson Button and I think it is awful that no famous

← **Ready to go in his karting overalls at the start of a career that would take him to the top.** LAT

11

← **Two-year-old Jenson pictured with his sisters (l to r) Samantha, Natasha and Tanya.**
📷 Rex Features

↙ **Jenson as a child with his father, John.**
📷 Rex Features

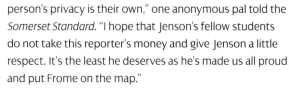

"YOU DON'T GET BORED WITH WINNING... COMING SECOND AND THIRD IS BORING, BUT NOT WINNING"

JENSON BUTTON

person's privacy is their own," one anonymous pal told the *Somerset Standard*. "I hope that Jenson's fellow students do not take this reporter's money and give Jenson a little respect. It's the least he deserves as he's made us all proud and put Frome on the map."

Jenson is remembered as a polite kid, pleasant and always smiling. And one who spent a lot of time karting. One of his teachers remembers him bringing his kart into school one morning as the centrepiece for the assembly. All the locals also knew him from the familiar Transit van which he and his father used to transport the kart to his various race meetings.

Jenson Button was born in Frome on January 19, 1980. He grew up with his three older sisters, Natasha, Samantha and Tanya. Shortly before his eighth birthday his parents separated. Afterwards his father John bought a kart from his old friend Keith Ripp, a former rallycross ace who'd built up a successful car performance accessory business. Not really knowing what the hell to do with it, John presented it to his son as a Christmas present. They took it for a preliminary test run on a disused airfield at Bridgwater. But Jenson soon tired of that and they decided to enter Jenson in his debut race at the Clay Pigeon track in Dorset, about an hour's drive from their Somerset home.

He won, first time out. At that time Jenson really thought it was just a bit of luck. But in reality, long before he even registered on the car racing fraternity's long-range radar screens, it would be his first step down a long road that would turn him into a seasoned and streetwise professional racer.

"It rained more or less all day," John Button says. "When he won, I did the unforgiveable thing of running out onto the track and jumping up and down. I soon learned."

Before long Jenson was making rapid progress through the ranks of championship karting, although resources were sometimes stretched. Most weekends they would set off for a meeting, and, as Button senior told Richard Williams of *The Guardian*, their return from one race in Scotland was only made possible when he borrowed enough money to fill the tank of his van for the journey home.

Jenson climbed up through the ranks with the support of both parents, but in particular his father, who bankrolled his efforts and prepared his karts. Although his parents had decided to go their separate ways, both they and Jenson's sisters always remained incredibly supportive of his efforts to make the motor racing big time.

Jenson has a fine competition pedigree behind him. His father John competed against Alexander Wurz's father on the European rallycross scene back in the late 1970s. Wurz would later race against Jenson's Williams from the cockpit of a Renault R200 F1 contender.

In 1991, Jenson moved up into the Cadet class. The category could only be described as a kart racing phenomenon. With some of the competitors barely within sight of their tenth birthday, the sight of a swarming pack of these pre-teenage hornets droning round in huge nose-to-tail bunches is as electrifying and intensely competitive as any F3 or Formula Ford competition.

Jenson took to it like a duck to water. In 1991, he won all 34 races in which he competed to win the British Cadet Championship. He also won the British Open title, and repeated that achievement in 1992 and 1993. In 1992 he also won the British Junior Championship.

"You don't get bored with winning," said Jenson years later as he reflected on his kart racing days. "Coming second and third is boring, but not winning." Yet sustaining one's competitive edge in any category of motorsport can be a difficult balancing act. You are under the spotlight to perform all the time and the intensity of that pressure can lead you to push just a bit too hard, and go over the edge.

It happened to Button in 1994 when he was leading the British Junior series. He destroyed his chances with a series of uncharacteristic accidents. On reflection, he acknowledges that he "lost his head a bit." That same year he raced in the World Championship event for the famous Italian Birel factory team, kart makers of distinction since the 1960s. Then, in 1995, with his parents' blessing, it was

↑ **Already showing a winning smile, Jenson poses for his school portrait.**
📷 Rex Features

← **Still wearing that smile, even though he's barely into his teens.**
📷 LAT

decided that Jenson would take the plunge and contest the Italian national championship as a professional.

"A lot of the big names in karting are from Italy," he says, "the teams, the chassis manufacturers and the engine specialists. So I went there to get to know everybody." Jenson's schooling became something of a problem, but the 14-year-old jetsetter managed to sustain some semblance of academic progress, aided by additional tuition at evening classes. Under the circumstances he was pretty successful, although he rather shamefacedly confessed that his Italian never progressed much beyond the language of the kart track pit lane.

Between winning the British Cadet Championship at 11 years old and the European Championship at 17, Jenson acquired a reasonably rounded education. Early in his racing career, his junior and middle-school classmates knew nothing of his sporting prowess. But by the time he arrived at Frome College to study for his GCSEs, it was impossible to disguise the reason for his absences.

"He kept the two worlds firmly separate," Dave Kitchener, his old form tutor, told *The Guardian*. "He was a regular member of the community, and that was why he was so well liked. If you asked him about what he was up to, he'd tell you. But there was no boasting or bragging."

Jenson was also suitably downbeat about his achievements. "At school I did well in French but I couldn't speak a word of it, so I really don't know how I did that and in Italy I picked up a bit of the language," he says. "I could

speak to the mechanics about the chassis but the biggest problem was that they all spoke English so it made it very difficult to learn Italian." Nevertheless, Button astounded the karting fraternity by winning the Italian title first time out, scoring twice as many points as the runner-up. In the World Championship he led most of the way but his tyres went off and he finished second.

It was inevitable that for 1996 Button would get a top drive and he was signed by the Team GKS using works Tecno-Rotax karts. He finished fifth in the European Formula A Championship and the team decided to put him into Formula Super A for 1997. The rest is history. "It was the Formula 1 of karting," Jenson explains, "and it is very professional compared to Formula Ford, for

example. People pay the same kind of money to race in Formula Ford."

In addition to the European title Button also won the Ayrton Senna Memorial Cup at Suzuka. "It is not automatically the winner of the race who wins the cup," he says. "They pick the driver that reminds them most of Senna and I was lucky enough to win it."

What he modestly keeps to himself is that in the pre-final race he started 18th and finished in the wheel tracks of the winner. He also makes no mention of the fact that he was fighting for the lead in the final when the chain on his kart snapped. The President of the International Karting Federation Ernest Buser was prompted to remark, "Jenson reminds me of Senna."

↑ **Learning his craft, Jenson (189) pilots his Tecno kart during the CIK-FIA World Championship Karting race at Valence, France in September 1995. Jenson went on to finish second in the race.**
📷 sutton-images.com

The problem with Jenson winning the European Championship at his first attempt was that there was precious little point in his staying in Formula Super A, so Button made the jump to car racing. By the end of 1997 he could look back with a huge sense of satisfaction. His achievements over the previous nine years had been remarkable. A generation earlier, any bright young talent seeking to cut a path through to a career as a professional racing driver would have had their hands full making any impact at all.

Button's achievement of taking the European Formula Super A series at his maiden attempt was a first; he was also the first British driver to take the crown as well as being the youngest ever to do it. In achieving this, the wide-eyed young Brit elevated himself onto a distinguished list of previous winners, which included Jarno Trulli, with whom he would later be partnered in the Renault F1 squad, and CART champion Alex Zanardi, ironically the man Button would take over from in the Williams Formula 1 team for the 2000 season.

Winning the European kart title involved competing in eight events. You had to demonstrate sufficient speed and race craft to fend off the opposition and the consistency and judgement to ensure that you're still running at the end. It may seem like stating the obvious, but striking such a successful balance has often proved beyond many who one might imagine would scale the sport's upper reaches if their merit was assessed on pure speed alone.

Karting, of course, is a split-second environment in which identifying the true future stars from those who are simply very good is an imprecise science. Some would say that luck and being in the right machinery at the right moment is the real key, but consistency is the crucial element that marks the genuine star apart.

During his climb to karting prominence, Jenson would also make the acquaintance of several other bright-eyed young chargers, all of whom wanted to make the big time and even dreamed that one day they might graduate to Formula 1. Most prominent among this elite group of Button's friends were Anthony Davidson, by 2004 running alongside Jenson in the BAR-Honda F1 team as third driver,

"WE WERE JUST KIDS, BUT WE WERE LEARNING TO BE COMPETITIVE"
JENSON BUTTON

and Dan Wheldon who is now one of the front runners in the Indy Racing League. "We always knew that one of us would make it big," says Davidson. "We just didn't know which one of us, but we thought it was just possible that we could all be there."

"We just had a feeling about making it a long time ago," adds Wheldon. "We knew we had talent and the things it would take. We were only eight, nine years old at the time but somehow we felt we knew. It's funny, but circumstances mean that we don't see each other that often anymore, but when we do it's like we've been together for ever. It takes us about five minutes to catch up."

"We were always beating each other and it was good fun," recalls Jenson. "We were friends, too, which made it nice. We were just kids, but we were learning to be competitive."

Now came a turning point. Jenson had reached the pinnacle of karting and would now have to move forward into cars. But to do that meant raising funds that were certainly beyond the means of John Button. Graduating into Formula Ford 1600 for 1998 was probably going to cost around £90,000. So unless John and Jenson could find some hard backing, and soon, the boy's racing career and

←← **One for the trophy cupboard. Jenson displays the spoils of victory at the 1995 *Autosport* Show.** 📷 LAT

← **Celebrating victory in the 1997 European Kart Championship.** 📷 LAT

↓ **Pushing hard during the fight for the 1997 European Kart Championship.** 📷 sutton-images.com

→ **Shaking hands with Bernie Ecclestone at the Spanish Grand Prix in 1998, the meeting at which a number of British Formula 1 journalists were introduced to Jenson for the first time.**
sutton-images.com

↓ **In action at Croft during the 1998 TOCA Slick 50 Formula Ford Championship. Jenson finished third in the race, behind Dan Wheldon and Marcos Ambrose in the works Van Diemens.**
LAT

↑ **Leading the rest of the pack on the opening lap at Snetterton. Jenson eventually finished second behind Dan Wheldon.**
📷 LAT

→ **August 1998, just four months into his Formula Ford career, and Jenson already looks more seasoned and mature.**
📷 sutton-images.com

lifelong hopes faced the very real danger of stalling in the pit lane.

Jenson's graduation from karting into the British FF1600 Championship took place in 1998. In fact he considered making the jump straight into F3, but resisted the temptation after discussions with David Robertson and Harald Huysman, both of whom were to be key players in shaping and organising his early career. Robertson, in particular, was a fan of Button's talent from an early age. He and his son Steve later discovered Kimi Räikkönen, of course, and subsequently lost their role as Button's managers to John Byfield of Essentially Sport.

In May 1998, in a restaurant in the centre of Barcelona, Huysman, a former Formula 3 driver, and a British businessman by the name of David Robertson introduced a small group of journalists to a slim, well groomed young man. He made an impact, but not that big an impact. He had a pleasant character, and looked you straight in the eye. But did he have what it takes to mark him out from

↑ **Jenson pushes hard on his way to a dominant pole position for the Formula Ford Eurocup race at Spa-Francorchamps in September 1998 – his first visit to the classic Belgian circuit. He finished fifth in the race after a spin.**

the rest of the ambitious young Brit pack, all aiming for the top, all determined to break into Formula 1?

That was the first meeting with Jenson Button for a number of British Formula 1 press corps. The only one who had really been keeping a close eye on him had been David Tremayne of *The Independent*, who had been alerted to his potential on the strength of his kart racing achievements. Tremayne would be as loyal an advocate of Button's cause over the next few years as the rest of us would be sceptics.

At the age of 18 Button had made the transition from karts to cars and found himself a shrewd management team in Huysman and the Robertsons. They invested heavily in Button's career in return for a 35 per cent share of his future income, and enlisted the help of Keith Sutton,

a motor racing photographer who had helped publicise Ayrton Senna's early career. In return for putting his agency's logo on Button's virgin-white car, Sutton used his contacts to spread the word about the young driver's talent.

It was Sutton who persuaded Bernie Ecclestone to grant Button a paddock pass for the Spanish Grand Prix in 1998. He also put together a sponsorship proposal when Button moved up to Formula 3 the following year, and helped attract Frank Williams's attention 18 months later when Alain Prost offered Button a test in his Formula 1 car, again at Barcelona.

David Robertson was rich, and a streetwise wheeler dealer with a roguish charm. His deep knowledge of

motorsport was buttressed by the achievements of his son Steve. The younger Robertson had raced competitively in the British Formula 3 Championship, handled a works Ford Mondeo in the British Touring Car Championship and also competed in the US with distinction, winning the 1994 Indy Lights Championship, the feeder series for Champcar. Huysman had also been an accomplished Formula 3 contender, so between them, the three men could deploy an outstanding blend of financial resource, racing savvy and business judgement.

David Robertson was keen to identify and bring on a new British talent. He fancied the challenge, the gamble, if you like, of investing in a new rising star, of having his judgement proved correct. It would also prove to be an

astute investment. Bankrolling a bright young star's entry to single-seater racing would require a significant cash investment. But with a multi-year management contract in place guaranteeing a healthy slice of that driver's income, maybe as much as 40 per cent for up to five years, if he made it into Formula 1, it would be jackpot time for Robertson and Huysman. But the real question was just who to back?

"Jenson was first brought to my attention by Harald," he says. "He had heard about him from some guy he knew in Belgium who was involved in karting and he reckoned Jenson was the best talent he'd seen since Ayrton Senna. Meanwhile I also spoke to Terry Fullerton, who was one of the handful of kart racers that Senna really rated. So all the

Buttons Jnr and Snr celebrate championship victory at Silverstone.
📷 sutton-images.com

Nose to nose with team-mate and title rival Derek Hayes at Brands Hatch in September 1998.
📷 LAT

evidence came together pointing to the fact that Jenson was the guy we should look after. By this stage Jenson had already been promised some funds from another source to go car racing, but it all fell through leaving him in limbo. So I put a call in to John Button, we had a brief chat and arranged to meet up. So that was basically when we put pen to paper and the moment was ripe for him to make the step forward into cars, which he did in 1998.

"Harald originally hadn't any intention of investing in Jenson," adds Robertson, "but he eventually came in, paid half and we committed to financing him through. My son Steve, who, of course, knows a lot about motor racing, told me I was mad, that the chances of getting Jenson through were pretty slim. I told him, well, I was going to take that chance, because if you think he's good enough – which Steve also clearly did – then I thought that we were good enough to get him there, because we knew motorsport pretty well."

Before racing in Formula Ford Button received his first taste of Formula 3 with a test of a 1997 Dallara, run by Carlin Motorsport, at the Pembrey circuit, near Llanelli, in south Wales. "It went very well," Jenson recalled to Joe Saward of the influential *grandprix.com* website. "Warren Hughes was testing at the same time with a Renault engine and a 1998-spec car and I did a time which was three tenths slower with an engine that was at the end of its mileage. I was very pleased. Actually I wasn't. At the time I was a bit disappointed because I don't like people going faster than me even if it was my first test in an F3 car. I was a bit down. Formula 3 seems to be a bit more interesting than Formula Ford although at that stage I hadn't actually raced an F3 car. It was easier to drive because there was a lot more grip and downforce and that is why the times are a lot closer. In Formula Ford you have no wings and so you slide."

For his part, Hughes was impressed. "To be in the ballpark immediately was extremely impressive on Jenson's part, irrespective of the comparative speed between us. He was extremely smooth and that would later come into much sharper perspective when Jenson did a full season of F3 in 1999. More than in most categories of racing, in F3 smoothness is the key. You have to apply controlled aggression, aggression to the point where you are not over-driving the car and losing speed. I think Jenson had that point well sussed from an early age."

Yet there was a huge risk involved in making the transition straight from karting to F3, even for a youngster of Button's undoubted potential. Learning how to drive a single seater effectively would be a big enough challenge in itself without grappling to make sense of slicks and aerodynamic downforce at the same time. Even the great Ayrton Senna progressed gradually through Formula Ford,

then FF2000 and into Formula 3 over the course of three seasons. That said, Steve Robertson, who made the trip to that Pembrey test, reported back that he was extremely impressed with Jenson's composure. His father David was keen that Jenson should make the big jump, but the teenager was reluctant to do so.

In the event, Button persuaded David Robertson that he should go into FF1600 with Jim Warren's Haywood Racing operation where he would be partnered by Derek Hayes and pitched up against some of his old karting rivals, most notably Dan Wheldon who was regarded as one of the pre-season favourites. Despite predictions that he was unlikely to be competitive in his first season of Formula Ford, and that Haywood's Mygale chassis would not be a match for the latest Van Diemen, Jenson made the transition with a seamless efficiency that may have surprised some observers but not those who'd been monitoring his progress in the world of karting.

Jenson finished third in his first race and quickly got into

"I WAITED FOR THE LAST FOUR MINUTES AND THEN WENT FOR IT AND I PUT THE CAR ON POLE, A TENTH OFF THE LAP RECORD."

JENSON BUTTON

the swing of things, mastering the subtle nuances of racing and qualifying technique with an assured confidence, even though the gamesmanship displayed by his rivals sometimes caught him by surprise. On his first outing at Silverstone, for example, he had problems in qualifying. "I had been quite fast in testing, so when I went out to qualify the first few laps were a nightmare because I had about six people behind me trying to see what I was doing and every lap I had people slowing down so they could get behind me and that was slowing me down," he says. "I came in after ten minutes and told the crew that there was no point in going out because I just could not get a good lap and that it was better to wait until the very end. I waited for the last four minutes and then went for it and I put the car on pole, a tenth off the lap record."

Under increasing pressure as the season wore on, Jenson survived some other instructive experiences including being excluded from a meeting at Brands Hatch after he'd overtaken Dan Wheldon under a yellow caution flag as they battled for the lead. Button explained that

← Spraying the champagne after victory in the Slick 50 Formula Ford Championship at Silverstone in September 1998. Jenson clinched the championship after finishing second in the first heat and then celebrated with a win in the second heat.

📷 sutton-images.com

→ The candidates for the 1998 BRDC McLaren *Autosport* Award pose in their competition overalls. The winner is beaming confidently second from the right.
📷 LAT

→→ An amazing moment with Steve Rider at the presentation of the 1998 BRDC McLaren *Autosport* Young Driver of the Year Award. The award kickstarted Jenson's F3 career.
📷 LAT

→ Getting his reward. Almost a year after winning the BRDC McLaren *Autosport* Award, Jenson tries his hand in a McLaren-Mercedes F1 car on a damp track at Silverstone. It is November 1999 and by now he has a year's experience in F3 under his belt.
📷 LAT

Wheldon's car had effectively masked his view of the flag and that he was unaware of his accidental transgression. He felt it was a bit much excluding him from the entire meeting, but he filed the experience away in his personal memory bank and learned from the experience.

Jenson's successful efforts in winning the TOCA Slick 50 Formula Ford 1600 Championship crown put him in pole position for the BRDC McLaren *Autosport* young driver of the year award. He also had a victory in the Brands Hatch Formula Ford Festival and runner-up status in the Euroseries to embellish his personal CV. With a cheque for £50,000, a test drive in a McLaren-Mercedes F1 car and sheafs of free publicity, this is the most coveted award a young driver can receive. By any standards, it is a sensational prize and involves a programme of detailed analysis, observation and assessment at a carefully structured test session held at Silverstone, the home of the BRDC.

In Jenson's year this involved first driving a Lotus Elise from the Silverstone Racing School. Then an F3 Dallara-Mugen provided by Alan Docking Racing, and finally a Nissan Primera touring car. Then the candidates were subjected to a videoed interview to test their social and communication skills. Then the judges decided that they wanted all the candidates to return again on another day and repeat the whole procedure again. Jenson would admit that he found the off-track interviews stressful, but intriguing. But he needn't have worried.

There was another highly respected racing personality who had no doubts about Button's potential from an early stage. This was John Fitzpatrick, BRDC club secretary and a member of the judging panel for the BRDC McLaren *Autosport* awards for many years in the 1990s. Speaking to the author shortly after Jenson bagged his first F1 pole position at Imola in 2004, he made it clear that the young British driver's progress had come as no surprise to him.

"I remember when he walked in the door of the BRDC suite on the first morning of the testing," said Fitzpatrick. "He looked like a winner, the way he carried himself and talked. Strange how you can tell before they even get into the car. As secretary of the BRDC, I was the organiser and chairman of the judges for the award from 1993 until 1999 when I left BRDC. I was one of five judges.

"It was a rule that the boys had to come alone, without parents or friends. The weather over the two days was atrocious and we had to schedule an extra day. In those circumstances you would have expected them to be a little nervous but Jenson was supremely confident and outstanding in the wet.

"In fact Nick Faldo, in one of his articles in *The Times* recently also quoted what I said about being able to assess a young driver before he even sat in the car, because he too, in his support of young golfers, said he was able to judge a young golfer by the way he walked on the tee and took his club out of the bag." And Jenson duly won the day, following in the wheel tracks of such celebrated names as David Coulthard and Dario Franchitti.

With his cheque for £50,000 safely tucked away as a deposit in preparation for the cost of a Formula 3 season, Button could really enjoy every second of his outing in a McLaren-Mercedes F1 car, a test that took place in the rather depressing surroundings of a wet Silverstone one dank morning in November 1999. The track was wet enough for rain tyres to be deployed, even though the track was starting to dry out by the time Jenson got into the swing of things. He completed his first ten-lap run and came into the pits to think things over. Then did just eight laps of his allotted second ten-lap stint before coming in and telling the team that, as the tyre treads were starting to chunk on the drying tarmac, he'd better call it a day there and then.

Dave Ryan, the McLaren team manager and a veteran of 24 years with the company, was impressed. Not so much with the speed and assurance which Jenson had demonstrated behind the wheel, but more by his assurance and general all-round polish. "The guy handled

himself incredibly well," Ryan told David Tremayne, "just the way he approached it, the way he drove the car. He used the radio and it just seemed natural to him. He told us what he was doing all the time."

[02]

THROUGH TO THE THRESHOLD OF F1

Jenson moved into Formula 3 in 1999 with the Silverstone-based Promatecme team, driving a Renault-engined Dallara, which wasn't the most competitive machine in the field. He finished third in the championship which was won by fellow Brit Marc Hynes. Yet it is testimony to the unpredictability of the motor racing business that Hynes's career effectively stalled thereafter and Button's accelerated towards the stars. What made the difference? Astute management, good contacts, or just the fact that Button was better?

Winning the British F3 Championship has historically opened doors to a Formula 1 test drive, or in recent years it at least ensured that the driver concerned was in the pound seats when it came to securing a Formula 3000 test drive. Yet the fact of the matter is that money talks. Button would benefit in this respect not simply from the fact that the Robertsons had backed his early progress with hard cash, but that they had an interest in ensuring he advanced up the ladder as quickly as was prudent in order to ensure a return on their investment.

The British F3 season basically came down to a tussle between Hynes, the 21-year-old from Gloucestershire, and Luciano Burti, the young Brazilian who would later join the Jaguar F1 team. Hynes had won the British Formula Renault title in 1997 driving for the Manor Motorsport team, then moved elsewhere for an unsuccessful maiden F3 season, before returning to the Manor operation when

it took the decision to move up a gear and graduate to F3 in 1999. Armed with the familiar Dallara chassis powered by a Mugen-Honda engine, Hynes got off to a flying start by winning the first two races. Later he added another three victories, including the British Grand Prix supporting race and the prestigious Marlboro Masters event at Zandvoort, the seaside circuit near Haarlem that used to host the Dutch Grand Prix.

Hynes was ranged against Burti who was driving for the blue riband Paul Stewart Racing operation. Burti struggled to get the best out of the Dallara F399 in the early races of the season and only really got things under control by late summer following an intensive programme of test and development work. Branded the best of the rest was Jenson, driving a Renault-engined Dallara for the Silverstone-based Promatecme team. The 19-year-old won three races and made plenty of mistakes, which reflected the fact that he was only two years out of kart racing, yet he managed to mark himself out as probably the best young driver on the UK Formula 3 starting grids.

It had been a long, hard winter. At the end of his Formula Ford season, there had been offers from at least two Formula 3 teams for him to race in the important Macau Grand Prix meeting in the Far East. Jenson declined the offers, flattered though he was, as he appreciated that this might be a little too over-optimistic a move to make at this stage of his career. But Keith Sutton was

← **A step up the ladder. Jenson moved into Formula 3 with the Promatecme team for 1999.**
📷 LAT

↑ **Jenson drove the Dallara-Renault to third place in the 1999 British F3 Championship.**
📷 LAT

↓ **Jenson's first F3 win. Thruxton, 11 April 1999.**
📷 LAT

monitoring the situation closely. For Jenson Button, the old adage that states it's not what you know but who you know was about to come true, and not for the first time in his career.

Sutton went to the final F3 meeting of the 1998 season and met up with Promatecme boss Serge Saulnier who he knew through his thriving Sutton Motorsport Images business, which was based in nearby Towcester. Keith had developed a keen feel for promising young drivers over the past couple of decades, from the time he homed in on Ayrton Senna's peerless genius when the Brazilian was

racing in FF2000 back in 1982. It was getting a bit late in the day to arrange a decent F3 drive for Jenson, but Sutton knew his stuff and was an ace salesman. He spoke to Saulnier and Tim Jackson, Renault UK's PR director. Saulnier was eventually bowled over by Sutton's sales pitch and offered to give Jenson a test outing at Magny-Cours.

Tim Jackson had made the point that it was Renault's general policy to support drivers who'd graduated from their junior formulae. But, for all that, he seemed quite open-minded towards Jenson. So he went to do the test at Magny-Cours and Saulnier was immediately impressed, noting the precision and accuracy with which Jenson picked up the racing lines even though he'd never driven at Magny-Cours before. By the end of the afternoon Saulnier made a commitment. He felt that in Jenson he'd just seen something extremely special, and he wasn't about to let him slip through his fingers. He wanted the 18-year-old to have the drive.

Button's outstanding potential and star quality went on immediate display. The opening round of the British F3 contest took place at Donington Park where Jenson displayed his in-bred car control by qualifying his Dallara-Renault on pole position in the soaking conditions. Things dried out for the race, which Hynes won by just under 4 seconds from Jenson and posted fastest lap to boot. Burti was third ahead of the promising Indian rising star Narain Karthikeyan.

Jenson could only finish sixth in round two at

Silverstone, but he held everybody's attention by posting his first F3 win at Thruxton in round three, trailed home by Paul Stewart runner Andrew Kirkcaldy with Hynes in third place. Button qualified second, and then stormed away to win. Marcus Simmons wrote in *Autocourse*: "This young man exudes star quality and, at the end of the season, was agonising over the tricky decision of whether to stay in F3 for a second season – for which he would be clear title favourite – or make an early step to Formula 3000."

With just three of the season's 16 races completed Jenson held second place in the British F3 Championship table with 43 points, just ten adrift of Marc Hynes. Yet Jenson could take nothing for granted. A fortnight later came the Brands Hatch 'double header' event where everything seemed to go wrong. He qualified fourth and fifth, and finished eighth and seventh in races won respectively by Luciano Burti and Narain Karthikeyan. Granted, Jenson had boosted his points total to 53, but Hynes – who'd finished third and sixth in the two events – now led the championship with 73 points; Burti's successes had vaulted him into second place ahead of the Promatecme driver on 57 points.

← **Celebrating after victory and fastest lap in the second race at Pembrey in August 1999.**
📷 sutton-images.com

⬇ **Into battle! Jenson's Promatecme Dallara-Renault takes up position on the front row of the grid, alongside Marc Hynes's Mugen-Honda-powered car at the British Grand Prix meeting in July 1999.**
📷 sutton-images.com

For Button, the overwhelming problem was the Renault engine's comparative lack of power when pitched against the rival Mugen-Honda propelled machines. Part of the problem seemed to stem from the fact that the preparation of the engines had been switched from Renault Sport to the specialist preparation company Sodemo. The resultant lack of straight line speed was painfully frustrating, but it was an instructive experience for Jenson in the sense that he quickly learned to control his disappointment and be very measured in his observations about the engine's shortcomings. After all, Saulnier had given him his chance to make the move up to F3, investing a great deal of confidence in his potential and Promatecme was the factory Renault representative in the British Championship.

Burti won again at Oulton Park, leading home the fast but inconsistent Danish driver Kristian Kolby by a couple of seconds with Matt Davies and Andrew Kirkcaldy next up before Jenson took the flag in fifth place, 5 seconds behind the winner. It was a strong performance at the challenging Cheshire parkland circuit, but the sense of expectancy generated by that early win obviously took some of the gloss off his achievement and the gaps separating the leading contenders in the British F3 series were obviously very close indeed.

At Croft in June Button failed to finish after the throttle stuck open; that was followed up with a sixth at Brands Hatch from third on the grid. The British Grand Prix supporting race at Silverstone was obviously a big deal

on to Snetterton, that bleak Norfolk airfield track far removed from the glitz and glamour of Silverstone at Grand Prix time. Button qualified fourth, but got carried away with the intensity of his battle for the lead against Burti and made a rare slip, spinning to the back of the field. After a long haul back through the field he gained a distant 11th place. Admittedly this netted him two valuable points, boosting his tally to 85, but Kristian Kolby was now only six points behind him in fifth place. If Jenson was to improve his position in the championship he needed to act fast.

Before the next F3 championship 'double header,' scheduled for the Pembrey track in West Wales on 15 August, Button took a trip across to Zandvoort for the prestigious one-off Marlboro Masters F3 classic the weekend immediately prior to the Welsh fixture. Hynes won again ahead of Germany's Thomas Mutsch, Etienne dan der Line and Christjian Albers; Button came fifth. But Pembrey marked the real turnaround in Jenson's British F3 fortunes. He finished second to Kolby in the first race, then won the second from pole position, setting the fastest race laps in both events. Burti now led the championship on 157 points, just two ahead of Hynes, with Button now firmly ensconced again in third place on 122. Jenson now seemed to have regained some worthwhile momentum and he sustained that through to the Donington Park fixture on 5 September where again he finished second to Hynes and ahead of Burti, edging him closer to the Brazilian in the battle for second place in the championship.

There followed a three-week break in the F3 schedule after which the competitors crossed the Channel yet again, this time for a round of the British Championship on the daunting swerves of Spa-Francorchamps. Less than a year later, Jenson would qualify third on the grid for the

← In action during the Macau Formula 3 Grand Prix in November 1999. Jenson finished second, behind Darren Manning.
📷 sutton-images.com

↑ Jenson with David Robertson (centre) and Harald Huysman at the 1999 Macau F3 Grand Prix.
📷 sutton-images.com

for the F3 brigade, but Marc Hynes had the measure of the opposition in qualifying, storming to pole position with Jenson claiming second place on the front row of the grid. Jenson made the best start and led the opening half lap as far as Vale before Hynes nipped past, in part due to Button's unfamiliarity with the technique of running quickly from a standing start on cold tyres. He kept up the pressure and finished just 0.4 seconds down at the chequered flag, having claimed the consolation of posting the fastest race lap of 109.896mph. It was a good showing by any standards, but Jenson had now dropped to fourth place in the championship standings. Hynes now led on 124 points from Burti (121), Karthikeyan (88) and Button (83).

A fortnight after the British GP the F3 title chase moved

Belgian Grand Prix in a Williams-BMW F1 car. But for the moment the challenge of the Fina F3 Masters event lay ahead around 14 gruelling laps of the spectacular 4.330-mile circuit. Superbly, Jenson qualified on pole with a lap of 114.464mph, but in the race he seemed initially to lack the sheer speed required to run with the leaders and had to settle for fourth, 6 seconds behind the victorious Burti.

Finally at Silverstone on 10 October Burti and Hynes tangled and Jenson managed to outbrake Matt Davies to take the lead and race home to post his third F3 victory of the season; he won by 6 seconds with Hynes recovering to finish third. Button was anxious to win again in the season finale at Thruxton on 17 October, but after a poor start from fourth on the grid he ran down in seventh place for the first few laps. He later tangled with Andrew Kirkcaldy, which resulted in his retirement from the race. Hynes emerged as F3 champion on 213 points ahead of Burti (209) and Jenson on 168.

After the European season ended Jenson made a trip to the Far East to contest both the Macau and Korean F3 Grands Prix. He finished second in both behind Darren Manning's Dallara-Toyota. On the face of it, Jenson's best route forward would be a second season in British F3 with championship victory firmly in his sights. But, as I said earlier, one of motorsport's most endearing qualities is its dramatic unpredictability. As Jenson would find out over the next couple of months.

By the end of the 1999 season Jenson had certainly made his mark in F3. He'd finished third in the British Championship despite running with a less powerful engine than his key rivals and he had earned himself a reputation as an immaculately smooth young driver. He made few unforced errors, thought things through clearly and didn't allow himself to get flustered under pressure. Yet, for all his proven prowess, the key question of where he went next weighed heavily on the Robertsons' shoulders. They had steered and funded his career so far to great effect, but the options facing them were now less clear cut. Should they try to cut a deal to move Button into Formula 3000? Or should they go for broke and encourage him to make the jump to Formula 1?

"At the end of the day we weren't exactly inundated with offers, but during his time in Formula 3 in 1999 we put together a package which ensured that the F1 teams were at all times aware of what he was up to. He did a great job in Formula Ford, but of course didn't have the most competitive engine in Formula 3. But we were still able to establish his reputation firmly in their eyes. We were able to say 'get in now, the boy's ready for F1'. So he got in the Prost and showed he was a natural.

"As far as McLaren was concerned, yes there was an opportunity, but I didn't like the terms and we turned it down. Stewart was the same, basically 'we want to own you,' and these terms were not satisfactory either. Of course these teams were not used to people turning them down so we weren't too popular, but I think they all appreciate now that we were probably right to turn them down. We just didn't see McLaren at that point in time, with the number of drivers they had at their disposal, as the right team . . . We believed we could get a better deal for him elsewhere."

On the face of it, for the Grand Prix hopeful a move into Formula 3000 seemed to be the most logical path. This series had turned up a good number of F1 competitors over the previous decade and a half, including Jean Alesi, Olivier Panis, Nick Heidfeld and Justin Wilson. The category had certainly developed into a fertile breeding ground

← Racing through the streets during the Korean F3 Grand Prix in November 1999.
📷 sutton-images.com

⬇ Letting his hair down in Korea, where Jenson finished second to Darren Manning in the high-profile F3 International.
📷 sutton-images.com

for new talent, but it was not without its shortcomings. Although the series featured as the main supporting event on the programme at most European grands prix, by the end of the 1990s there were lingering doubts about the strength in depth of its competition. It was also shaded by F1 in the sense that anybody wanting commercial exposure in motorsport was more likely to be attracted by the sponsorship possibilities available in the Grand Prix paddock rather than committing their investment to a category with a second-class image.

Button and his managers decided to take things carefully. They knew it would be wise to take a long look at Formula 3000, but they were not totally convinced. Jenson was invited down to the Jerez track in the autumn of 1999 where he tested F3000 cars fielded by two of the

most experienced teams in the business, Super Nova and Fortec. He was suitably competitive and performed well, but he felt the cars were a little on the heavy side and the drop-off in performance as the tyres wore down was also a little frustrating. Jenson and the Robertsons also knew that if you didn't get into the right team at the right time, with the right budget and the best engineer, the chances of being eclipsed by ostensibly more talented drivers was a big risk indeed.

Yet another opportunity would present itself. Harald Huysman and the Robertsons were put in touch with Alain Prost who'd heard what a good job Jenson had been doing in F3. They met at Monza during the 1999 Italian Grand Prix weekend where the French team boss offered Jenson a test in one of his cars at Barcelona's Circuit de Catalunya. They moved carefully at first, grateful for the offer. But while they had total confidence in Jenson's ability to handle the situation, it was made clear to Prost that they were not prepared to sign any sort of conditional long-term option that might bind Jenson to the team beyond this one-off outing.

Many team principals would have brought negotiations to a halt there and then. Offering a test drive in exchange for first call on the services of a promising young driver was a technique well established in F1 circles and, taken at face value, it seemed extremely reasonable. With the on-track running costs of an F1 car approaching $1,500 a lap at the time Jenson was offered the Prost drive, it seemed

an understandable *quid pro quo* for the team owner to take an option on the driver's services. After all, if the team was to be responsible for promoting the career of a future Grand Prix winner then they deserved to reap the benefit. But Prost did not insist on such a commitment, something for which Jenson and his management team would be eternally grateful.

Button flew back from a holiday in Mexico to test the Prost, taking over the programme from regular team driver Jean Alesi, himself no mean F1 performer. The young Englishman adapted immediately and seamlessly to the challenge of operating a 3-litre Grand Prix car. He was instantly on the pace, handling the Prost with a decisive familiarity that had the pit crew mentally confused for a few seconds, almost forgetting that Alesi hadn't in fact stayed on to continue driving the car for another day.

The figures were impressive. Alesi had lapped in a best time of 1min 24.8sec after two days of testing at Barcelona. Then Jenson had a day to himself running with a comparable fuel load to that used when the Frenchman had been running. He was also using the tyres Alesi had used the previous day. Encouraged simply to go out and find his feet, Jenson was told that if he got into the 1min 28sec bracket by the end of the day, he would be doing well. Within five flying laps he'd done a 1min 26.8sec. He came into the pit lane and had a think about things. Then he did another six-lap run and topped it off with a 1min 24.4sec best.

Seasoned engineer Humphrey Corbett was working for Prost on Button's car that day and was dazzled by what he saw. "I can remember being incredibly impressed at the end of the day," said Corbett in 2004, by which time he was working as race engineer on the Toyota TF104 being raced by Olivier Panis. "Immediately he was within a second of our regular driver Jean Alesi. We thought 'Bloody hell, who is this guy?' He wasn't flustered, he was so relaxed and his feedback was very good. It was as if the guy had driven F1 for five years."

By this stage in his career Alesi was a seasoned and experienced campaigner, well versed in the ebb and flow of F1 fortune. By the time he'd signed for the Prost team, most agreed that the popular French driver's golden days were behind him, but he always retained an honest and open mind when it came to assessing emergent new talent. Alesi might not have been the most successful of drivers in F1, but he was certainly among the most generous-spirited. And he could see Button's potential as a driver while fully understanding the potential pitfalls which might stand in his way as he tried to reach the big time.

"IMMEDIATELY HE WAS WITHIN A SECOND OF OUR REGULAR DRIVER JEAN ALESI. WE THOUGHT 'BLOODY HELL, WHO IS THIS GUY?'"

HUMPHREY CORBETT – PROST ENGINEER

← ↓ Jenson's first serious test in an F1 car came at Barcelona in the Prost AP02-Peugeot. The level of confidence and assurance he displayed amazed the French team.

📷 sutton-images.com

"I saw his speed straight away", Alesi recalled ten years later, "and I thought, 'He's the next one.' And in his first season he was very good. But things went wrong which were not necessarily his fault.

"It happened to me, too. You make some decisions that might not be the right ones and also things happen that are not in your control. And then your results are not good, but people don't understand why. So when I finally won my first race, it was not a pleasure. It was deliverance. And I'm sure that's how Jenson felt."

It took Button six years to win his first Grand Prix, then another two and a half seasons and 40 more races before he won a second. Throughout 2007 and 2008 he scored a total of nine championship points, while Lewis Hamilton, five years his junior, swept into Formula One and roared to the world title. Maurice Hamilton wrote in *The Observer*; "Button's absolute refusal to complain made a profound impression on those who recognised the true dimension of his talent."

"What is happening to him now is exactly what he deserves," Alesi added. "Through all the hard times he's had, he never tried to blame anyone else. That shows what a good character he's got."

↑ **Jenson talks to Williams engineers in the garage at Jerez in January 2000...**

↓ **...before heading on to the track in a Wiliams-BMW for the first time.**
📷 Both LAT

Yet although Button was impressive, Prost had other problems on his hands simply keeping the team afloat. Cashflow rather than promising young drivers was the real priority. So Jenson watched and waited, wondering whether he might not have to complete a second year in Formula 3 in order to consolidate his reputation. His anxiety was heightened very slightly when he heard that Darren Manning had been approached by Williams after winning the two end-of-season F3 classics in Macau and Korea, races in which Button chased him home to post a couple of second places. As Jenson told David Tremayne, by this stage it almost seemed as though he'd become the victim of his own success. Ignoring the fact that Manning had benefited from a powerful Toyota engine in those two Far East races, if Button was so clever, said the logic, then this chap Manning must be even better. But there was more to it than that. Williams had met Darren before when he'd been short-listed for a Renault drive in the BTCC with Williams Touring Car Engineering, so he was already on Frank's radar screen.

The F1 grapevine is always alert, alive and vibrant. Within days of Button's test in the Prost the gossip began to do the rounds. David Robertson phoned Jim Wright, the Williams team's marketing director, with news of the Prost test. Wright was impressed, but wanted to be sure of the details before he communicated the facts to Frank Williams. Frank wasn't an easy man to impress and any hint that a third party might be hustling him into a deal had historically been met with indifference. One only had to look at his track record. In 1992 he'd run out of patience and withdrawn from further negotiations with the newly crowned World Champion Nigel Mansell. That decision led to Mansell leaving F1 and moving to the US where he won the CART championship the following year. Four years later, in 1996, Frank similarly withdrew from negotiations with Damon Hill for an extension of the British driver's contract as Hill was poised to win the title. Williams felt he was being hustled and responded accordingly.

A couple of weeks later Frank telephoned the young British driver. Jenson could hardly believe what he was hearing when he received a telephone call from Frank Williams expressing interest in his services. "I was having a drink with a few friends just before Christmas when my mobile rang and the voice at the end of the line said it was Frank Williams," he said. "I immediately suspected it was somebody playing a joke, but Frank said he just wanted to touch base with me and he later 'phoned back with the offer of a test drive."

Frank had already done a great deal of homework. He'd telephoned Harald Huysman at his office in Oslo and quizzed him in great detail about the Prost test, running through the whole thing almost lap by lap. In particular, he wanted to be sure about the fuel load Jenson had been running as that was the true key to the comparative performance against Alesi. If it transpired that Jenson had been running with a lighter car than the Frenchman, the comparison would have been distorted. If Williams was going to give Button a test run, he had to be sure. Huysman corroborated all the initial evidence. The signs were that Jenson's performance had been geuinely spectacular. As a result, on 13 January 2000, Jenson arrived at the Jerez circuit in southern Spain. He would have a run in the interim Williams FW21B development car. It had one of the previous year's chassis which had raced with a Supertec engine installed but now equipped with one of the first of the new BMW E41 V10s.

Williams was impressed with Button's personality, but decided to check out those impressions with BMW's newly appointed competitions manager Gerhard Berger. Gerhard confessed that he judged Button an interesting character and was keen to give him a run. But he was more impressed than even he could ever have anticipated after Jenson's first test at Jerez.

"What you've got to remember is that I knew Jerez extremely well, having driven my last Grand Prix there in 1997," he said, "so I knew instantly what I was looking for when I went up to the top of the control tower and watched Jenson lapping the circuit.

"It was quite incredible. He'd not driven an F1 car before, but he was instantly on the line, never ran wide, and the only indication that he was pushing hard came from the occasional locked brake as he probed the limit. It was obvious that he was an instinctive driver."

Yet to some extent the Jerez test was inconclusive. The new BMW engine wasn't reliable enough to give the new boy a sufficiently consistent run to be able to come to a fair conclusion. Yet time constraints were crowding

"I WAS HAVING A DRINK WITH A FEW FRIENDS JUST BEFORE CHRISTMAS WHEN MY MOBILE RANG AND THE VOICE AT THE END OF THE LINE SAID IT WAS FRANK WILLIAMS"

JENSON BUTTON

in on the Williams team. The launch of the new Williams-BMW FW22, together with the team's new sponsorship package from Compaq, was due to be unveiled to the press at Barcelona on 24 January. But there was another driver in the frame for the drive, a young Brazilian called Bruno Junqueira. The sponsorship link between the Brazilian fuel company Petrobras and Williams had brought Junqueira into the Grove camp as a test driver. He had also made quite a name for himself in the 1999 Formula 3000 championship, which was won by the German driver Nick Heidfeld.

As the *Autocourse* annual recorded in its annual review written by Simon Arron, "Brazilian Bruno Junqueira (Petrobras) is already favoured to succeed Heidfeld after a slightly rough-and-tumble season that underlined his searing pace and adventurous racecraft. His lone win, at Hockenheim, was just reward after he zipped past team-mate Max Wilson at about 170mph, with two wheels on the grass. It was one hell of a move and, to many, he was the revelation of the season. A few too many scrapes scotched his title chances, but it was an impressive year nonetheless."

Once the decision had been made to ditch Zanardi, it was inevitable that Junqueira would be a candidate for the vacant drive. Bruno was more experienced than Button, but there seemed little doubt that the British F3 graduate would offer more long-term potential. Even so, it was a risk. The pressure ramped up on the two men

when Frank Williams decided the only way to resolve the situation was a 'shoot out' between the two men at the Circuit de Catalunya on 23 January, the eve of the official announcement.

Jim Wright, the Williams team's head of marketing, takes up the story. "It was obviously going to be close because while Jenson had obviously been impressive in the Prost test, Junqueira was a very good driver, very quiet and methodical, and he'd already had a fair deal of mileage in the car," he recalled. "But come the shoot-out there was precious little to choose between them. The lap times were pretty well identical. Frank came onto me and said 'We can't make a decision. We need more time. It's just too close between them. You'll only be able to announce Ralf as one confirmed driver tomorrow and we'll just have to explain that the second driver will be one of these two other guys.'

"So we got ourselves organised to do just that, complete with supplies of media packs on both Jenson and Bruno and that was how we were going to do it. Then on the morning of the announcement, Frank called me from his car on the way into the circuit, with just 15 minutes left before the media conference was scheduled to begin and said 'Jimmy, we've decided to go with Jenson." So it is absolutely true that Jenson didn't know until ten minutes before the announcement. But Frank absolutely insisted on seeing Bruno first to explain that he hadn't got the drive, but it had been very close, and that he would be giving him a test driving contract."

Junqueira continued in F3000 through the 2000 season and ended up winning the championship. He contained his disappointment over not getting the Williams drive pretty well, even though he eventually had to switch to the CART series in North America to sustain his career in the longer term. "Racing in Formula 1 has always been my dream," he said during the summer of 2000. "That's not something I want to give up on. But as the season went on, more and more people kept saying to me 'Look, you might be better off trying to do something else if there are no decent drives available'. The more I thought about it, the more I began to see their point of view."

So Frank made his decision in Button's favour on the day of the official unveiling of the Williams FW22. BBC Radio Five Live radio commentator Jonathan Ledgard recalls being beckoned over for a word with Frank only minutes before the official announcement was due to be made.

The popular and enthusiastic Ledgard thought he was about to get the scoop of the F1 season, albeit by only a few minutes. He squatted down close to Williams's face. "Tell me, Jonathan," asked Frank with some gravitas, "when is the BBC going to get rid of Alan Hansen from its football commentaries? I can't understand a word he says . . ."

Jenson got the drive and immediately began to impress most observers with his obvious talent. Yet he was under absolutely no illusions. There had been no prevaricating whatsoever on Frank's part. Jenson knew that he would have to perform sensationally well if he was going to keep Juan-Pablo Montoya out of the Williams line-up.

The decision to plump for Montoya for 2001 was eventually formalised at around the time of the Monaco Grand Prix where Frank played absolutely straight with Jenson. He'd signed the young British driver on a five-year contract, so now it was a question of which team he would 'sub let' Button out to for the next few years. It turned out to be the Benetton – soon to be Renault – F1 squad.

⬇ **Ralf and Jenson pose, rather stiltedly, at the official launch of the Williams FW22 in January 2000.**
📷 LAT

➜ **Jenson looks pensive after parking up in the gravel trap during testing at Kyalami in February 2000.**
📷 LAT

[03]

HOPES RAISED AND DASHED

I f Jenson Button had arrived at Williams a year later, or indeed stayed with the team for a second straight season, things might have worked out very differently. From the touchlines there was the feeling that they were made for each other. The young British star, melding great natural flair with a huge willingness to learn, seemed just the sort of character to catch Frank Williams's imagination.

Yet by the same token, there was a willfully perverse streak to the Williams rationale. Perhaps it might be better described as attractively idiosyncratic. In a sense, it always seemed that they wanted whatever driver they hadn't got. In 1999 Frank had made the curious decision to sign the Indycar champion Alex Zanardi alongside Ralf Schumacher as part of a package which saw both Jacques Villeneuve and Heinz-Harald Frentzen being shown the door. Changing drivers is always a gamble, but changing both of them at once tends to damage a team's equilibrium, no matter how well-intentioned the decision.

So it proved for Williams, yet when the team seemed nicely settled with Button and Ralf Schumacher in 2000, all they could think about was bringing in Juan Pablo Montoya, the highly gifted and obviously hugely talented Colombian, for 2001. It seemed as though they were running ahead of events to no good purpose.

Williams was a team in transition at the start of the 2000 season. The great days of their partnership with Renault, which had delivered four Drivers' World Championships

between 1992 and 1997, were now disappearing in their personal rear-view mirrors. They had spent the 1998 and 1999 seasons wrestling with leased Supertec V10 engines – fixed specification versions of the once-great Renault V10s – but now they had cut a fresh deal with BMW, an in-depth technical collaboration designed to endure on a long-term basis.

"In September 1999 we produced an FW21B development car for the new engine," explained Williams Technical Director Patrick Head. "This basically had the suspension from the 1999 car (the FW21) and the 'Step 3' version of the new BMW engine, which was installed in the chassis with the oil tank ahead of the engine rather than in with the gearbox. This produced an oil system problem which, in fact, had a relatively simple solution but took a bit of time to sort out as it only arose when the engine was installed in the car rather than operating on the dynamometer."

The new FW22 was ready well ahead of the first race of the season, its design philosophy being to flatter the strong points of the FW21. At the same time Head's team had worked hard to eliminate some of its areas of weakness, most notably its poor aerodynamic performance on low downforce circuits. To get the best out of the new BMW type E4 engine it was also fitted with a seven-speed longitudinal gearbox rather than the six-speed transmission used on the 1999 car.

← **The big time! Jenson strolls confidently through the paddock, a Formula 1 driver at last.**
📷 LAT

→ **Making his reputation. Jenson at speed in the Willams-BMW FW22 during his freshman F1 season – seen here at the French Grand Prix in July 2000.**
📷 LAT

← Countdown to his first F1 race. Jenson sits with Williams Technical Director Patrick Head in the paddock at Melbourne prior to the 2000 Australian Grand Prix.

LAT

Of course, such considerations were almost of secondary importance to Jenson as the bare fact was that he was now an F1 driver. Sitting strapped in his FW22 as he waited in the pit lane at Melbourne on 10 March, poised to start first practice for the Australian Grand Prix, if he found it hard to take everything in, he certainly concealed any mounting apprehension.

Suddenly the signal was given and he was accelerating out onto the circuit close behind Michael Schumacher, one of his great heroes, at the wheel of his scarlet Ferrari. Yet the sun went in abruptly. Jenson spun into the wall during that Friday free practice session. Frank Williams accepted the new boy's slip with impassive equanimity. He appreciated the pressures involved. But that didn't alter the fact that Frank and Patrick Head had a deeply ingrained sense of disapproval when it came to drivers – particularly young and inexperienced drivers – crashing their cars.

On the second day things didn't get any better for Jenson. He had to abandon his repaired race car due to fuel pressure problems. Instead, he took over the spare Williams FW22, but a 'red flag' period scuppered his qualifying efforts. He would line up for his first Grand Prix start 21st on the grid. Only the little known Argentine driver Gaston Mazzacane would be behind him in the struggling Minardi M02.

At the end of the race he would be moderately satisfied. Not with his result, of course, because he failed to finish

due to an engine failure after 46 of the race's 56 laps. But it had been a bold and confident debut. Jenson had driven very tidily, making up places during a fraught opening lap to come round in 15th place.

"My start wasn't the best in the world," said Button, "but some people made worse getaways so it wasn't too bad. My first lap was very hectic and I tried to stay out of trouble. It was a nice steady race apart from a little mistake on the fifth lap. I just wish it had lasted another 20 laps."

The second round of the championship took place at Sao Paulo's ramshackle Interlagos circuit on 25 March. The

⬇ An unfortunate moment. Jenson spun into the wall during first practice for his maiden Grand Prix. Fortunately the crumpled Williams FW22 was repairable.

LAT

momentum seemed with him. He qualified ninth, two places ahead of his more seasoned team-mate Ralf Schumacher. He achieved this despite the need for an engine change between the Saturday morning free practice session and qualifying. Jenson was clearly getting the hang of the Formula 1 business.

In the race he would excel again, scoring his first championship point for sixth place after David Coulthard's McLaren-Mercedes was excluded from second place behind Michael Schumacher's winning Ferrari due to an infringement of the rules relating to the car's front wing endplates.

It was the overall quality of Jenson's driving which again attracted attention rather than the seventh place finish, which was magically transformed into sixth through circumstances beyond his own control. He'd fluffed his start, dropping from ninth to 14th by the end of the opening lap, but from then on it was a case of onwards and upwards.

For many laps Jenson was locked in a wheel-to-wheel battle with the highly experienced Jos Verstappen's Arrows A21, eventually slicing a confident path ahead of the Dutchman on lap 56. It was a small, but significant step along the road to Button's maturity. Here on that bumpy undulating circuit that had given so much to F1 history, where memories of epic days involving the Fittipaldi brothers, Carlos Pace, Ayrton Senna and many, many more, Jenson scored his first crucial championship point. Even at this early stage, it was clear that it wouldn't be his last.

The main rump of the European F1 season was next on the agenda, that helter-skelter of intense racing which starts in the early spring and runs pretty well through to the end of September. This is a particularly high pressure period for the competing teams as the relentless inevitability of the racing schedule makes it extremely demanding when it comes to developing the cars. The Williams-BMW FW22 was very much an experimental car in an experimental season. Williams and the German car manufacturer had been working behind the scenes for a couple of years, but there was nothing like proper race action to highlight the weaknesses within the new alliance.

For the San Marino Grand Prix at Imola things were looking up, at least for Ralf Schumacher. He qualified his FW22 fifth fastest in 1min 25.871sec. That was a second shy of Mika Häkkinen's pole position with the McLaren-Mercedes MP4/15, but it wasn't a bad show considering just how young the Williams-BMW partnership really was. Unfortunately Jenson made heavy weather of the qualifying session here at the evocatively titled Autodromo Enzo e Dino Ferrari. He couldn't quite get himself into the swing of manhandling his car – brutally, it seemed to him – over the punishing high kerbs. That's all part of the art of squeezing a quick lap out of the Imola circuit and he paid the price by lining up a distant 18th on the grid on 1min 27.135sec.

Jenson's maiden British Grand Prix was always going to be something of an emotional occasion, but to experience that feeling so early in his first F1 season was certainly something of an historic surprise. In 2000 some pseudo-political juggling with the F1 international calendar meant that the race at Silverstone would take place on an unseasonably early Easter Monday rather than its traditional July date when there would have been a chance of much better weather.

As it was, the weather dealt a terrible blow to Button's Silverstone debut. Heavy rain for much of the previous fortnight produced depressing scenes with paying spectators up to their ankles in glutinous mud, their cars bogged down up to their axles. It was all extremely depressing and the public car parks had to be closed on the Saturday in a bid to make things halfway reasonable in time for race morning. On the Sunday morning things got even worse. The combination of a capacity crowd and the painfully slow process of gaining access to the spectator car parks caused gridlock around the Northamptonshire circuit. Despite warnings from the police not to join the 15-mile traffic jams leading to the circuit, the 60,000-plus crowd displayed remarkable grit and determination. The venue, after all, looked more like the Glastonbury Festival than the British round of a five-star international motorsport.

Once trackside, the sodden fans wanted to be cheered up. Jenson did just that, qualifying a staggering sixth, one place behind Michael Schumacher's Ferrari, but crucially one place ahead of his team-mate Ralf. Come the race the fans were paid back for their discomfort and inconvienience. At the head of the pack David Coulthard stormed to an enormously popular win in the McLaren,

↑ **The two Williams-BMWs in close formation during the unseasonably early 2000 British Grand Prix at Silverstone held on Easter Sunday. Ralf and Jenson finished fourth and fifth.**
📷 LAT

← **Jenson meets the fans at Silverstone where he impressed everybody in the paddock with that fifth place.**
📷 LAT

→ The Ralf and Jenson show. Button couldn't initially match Ralf's pace, but by the second half of the season his speed was seriously rattling his more experienced rival.
📷 LAT

⬇ A chaotic scene at the 2000 Monaco Grand Prix after Jenson tipped Pedro de la Rosa into a spin, causing the race to be stopped.
📷 sutton-images.com

while Jenson, who'd run ahead of Ralf until the first round of refuelling stops, stormed home fifth. Both FW22s were misfiring badly in the closing stages of the race and, as it subsequently transpired, were remarkably fortunate to make it to the chequered flag. Jenson also produced the seventh fastest lap of the afternoon in what was a very convincing performance.

At the Spanish Grand Prix in Barcelona most of the media focus was on David Coulthard, who had survived a private jet accident the previous week at Lyons airport in which both the pilots died. It was probably just as well, as Button qualified a disappointing 11th, complaining that his FW22 seemed unduly affected by the crosswinds. Come the race, though, he drove well. He worked his way steadily through to sixth place before hopes of adding to his World Championship points tally were scuppered by an engine failure with four laps to go. Ralf finished fifth.

Button's first visit to Monaco was fraught with difficulties. Williams team insiders were impressed with the assured manner with which he tackled the unforgiving 2.094-mile ribbon of tarmac through some of the most expensive real estate on the planet. But his qualifying effort certainly didn't reflect the obvious energy and poise that was being deployed in the cockpit of Williams's number 10 car. When Eddie Irvine's Jaguar was limping home after suffering power steering failure, the flurry of yellow warning flags saw Jenson ease off the throttle on what he hoped would be his best qualifying lap. He ended up 14th on the grid, five places behind Ralf Schumacher. It wasn't any consolation when he heard Ralf complaining that Irvine had got in his way on his best lap as well.

The race start was dramatic. Initially Pedro Diniz, who had qualified his Sauber C19 in 19th place, was left stranded in the middle of the pack as the field accelerated away on the formation lap. It seemed as though the Brazilian was destined to start from the back of the grid, but as the pack stopped on the grid proper, Alex Wurz's Benetton suffered an engine failure. Race officials immediately aborted the start.

When the race finally got underway, Michael Schumacher's Ferrari accelerated into the lead. But an electrical problem with the race timing computer triggered the 'abort start' procedure and red warning strips appeared on all the teams' timing screens. Unfortunately, red flags weren't immediately waved around the circuit, so the pack roared onwards around what it thought was the opening lap. At the ultra-tight Loews hairpin, Pedro de la Rosa attempted to squeeze his Arrows around the outside of Button's Williams and the end result saw Jenson inadvertently tapping the Spaniard into a spin. The two cars shuddered to a halt, blocking the circuit, and the race was stopped.

Jenson jogged back to the pits to take over the spare Williams FW22. While running in 19th place after 17 laps his first Monaco Grand Prix ended when he pulled into the pits and retired with fluctuating oil pressure.

Button would press Ralf Schumacher pretty hard in the closing stages of the 2000 season, but it wasn't enough to keep his drive. The shaping of his immediate career prospects had been finalised long before the end of the 2000 season. The team was unquestionably impressed with Juan Pablo Montoya, and Frank was determined to get him on the payroll.

At the 2000 Canadian Grand Prix, David Robertson finally decided that he had to press Frank Williams on the issue of whether or not Jenson would be kept on the BMW Williams race team the following year.

"Yes, we went into the Williams deal knowing there was a possibility that Montoya would be considered for 2001,

> ## "JENSON WANTED TO STAY WITH WILLIAMS, BUT I KNEW FRANK HAD THIS DECISION TO MAKE [ABOUT MONTOYA]"
> **DAVID ROBERTSON**

but we negotiated an agreement to take care of that and it was the first time it had been done," he said. "If you talk to all these teams now you'll find, for example, teams like Renault have an interest in the driver. Frank had to pay him until he no longer wanted him, so knowing that he was going to take Montoya on he still paid Jenson and we were able to negotiate for his [Jenson's] salary elsewhere, which was a unique situation.

"Jenson wanted to stay with Williams, but I knew Frank had this decision to make [about Montoya]. But he was reluctant to tell me. So I went direct to him and said 'Frank, please tell me, am I free to talk to another team?' He told me I could, so I knew that the deal was done. So from then on I went out and made myself busy, basically."

While the astute Roberston was formulating the next step in his negotiating strategy, Button had a disappointing Canadian Grand Prix. Bugged by fuel pick-up problems he qualified a distant 18th. In the race itself, he trailed home 11th.

Frank Williams made the dilemma clear. "We had the choice between Jenson and Juan Pablo," he explained. "But we inclined towards Juan simply because he'd spent

↑**Despite starting from the back of the grid for the 2000 German Grand Prix at Hockenheim, Jenson stormed through the field, passing Mika Salo's Sauber for fourth place with two laps to go.**
📷 LAT

→ **During the build-up to the 2000 Malaysian Grand Prix, Jenson found time to relax away from the pressures of the on-track action.**
📷 sutton-images.com

two years in 900bhp Indycars and was further down his career development path than Jenson, if you like. In any case, we would have lost our option on his services if we hadn't taken up the chance of bringing him back to the F1 team. He knew that, Jenson knew that and it certainly wasn't a negative reflection on Jenson. He just didn't have the experience to match Juan Pablo, but he was clearly hugely talented."

After their trip across the Atlantic, the F1 teams returned to Europe to pick up the threads of the championship programme. The next race was the Austrian Grand Prix at the A1-Ring where the Michelin-shod Williams FW22s demonstrated their aversion to low-grip track surfaces. Button and Ralf Schumacher qualified 18th and 19th. In the race Button kept out of trouble to finish in an excellent fifth place, only just losing out in a battle for fourth with Jacques Villeneuve's BAR-Honda. He would come to know a lot more about Villeneuve in the years ahead.

"It was a hard race," said Jenson. "The first corner was pretty tough to find a way through and I'm not sure how I came out of it at the end. The team did a good job with my pit stop, but unfortunately Jacques was just able to pop out of the pits ahead of me."

By this time there was much media speculation that Button would be dropped by Williams at the end of the season. On the face of it, this was another case of Frank Williams getting shot of Britain's latest F1 super-hero in the

same way as he'd apparently ditched the legendary Nigel Mansell at the end of 1992. But, of course, there was more to this business than met the eye.

The subtleties of Jenson's contract had not been shared with the media and the situation looked slightly confused, certainly from the touchlines. In a sense this was compounded by what some observers saw as a mid-season dip in Jenson's performance. In reality, this was a by-product of his over-ambitious experimentation with his car's set-up combined with the fact that BMW had detuned its V10 engines in the interests of mechanical longevity.

But at Hockenheim, Jenson got his personal development curve back on track. Despite having to start the German Grand Prix from the back of the grid after his car refused to fire up prior to the formation lap, he stormed through to fourth at the chequered flag. This flawless drive was strategically abetted by two perfectly timed stops on laps 27 and 34, making the switch to rain tyres on the second pit visit.

"The team made an excellent job calling me in at the right time to switch to wet tyres," said Jenson. "It was very difficult to drive at that moment, because at the back of the circuit it was dry and in the pit lane it was raining. It was also a very exciting moment when I passed Mika Salo's Sauber to take fourth just two laps from the end of the race."

Patrick Head, seldom easily impressed, added, "It was a brilliant result for Jenson." It was also timely. At the

Hungarian Grand Prix a fortnight later it was confirmed that he would, after all, be staying in F1 for the 2001 season, with the Renault team.

By the middle of August 2000, Jenson's F1 future for the next two seasons had been successfully secured. David Robertson finalised a deal with Flavio Briatore for him to drive alongside Giancarlo Fisichella in the Benetton F1 squad starting with the first race of 2001. The arrangement gave Williams the option to claim him back as one of their race drivers for 2003 if Frank and Patrick Head felt so inclined.

Button radiated confidence when quizzed about his planned move. "I felt Benetton offered me the best opportunity of doing what I want above all else, to win races," he said. "I genuinely believe that Benetton will be challenging for victories over the next couple of seasons because I know what it has planned. I am fully aware of its commitment, and it certainly has the people, skill and resources to be successful. I will do my best to repay Flavio for the faith he has shown in me. If that means beating Williams in the process, so be it. Frank Williams would expect no other attitude from me."

Briatore, a hard nosed wheeler dealer who had helped shape Michael Schumacher's early career with Benetton, had been impressed with Button during his freshman year in F1. Privately, though, he was a little concerned with Jenson's image as a bit of a playboy. This derived largely from the image of him schmoozing his close pals on his luxury yacht 'Little Missie', which was moored alongside the paddock during the 2000 Monaco Grand Prix weekend. Yet Briatore was astute enough to see past that. He knew that Jenson had talent and could understand that a young man suddenly propelled into this world of wealth and conspicuous consumption would be keen to have a good time.

Many years later, at the dawn of his 2009 title challenge, Button would reflect on this period of his life with pin-sharp clarity. There were suggestions that he was immature and even just too damned pleasant to be a success. Suggesting that an F1 driver is too easy going is almost as negative as hinting that he lacks that most crucial stock-in-trade, the speed to get the job done. Yet it was all water off a duck's back to the young man from Frome.

"I never let those comments get to me, even during my lowest periods," he said. "It just made me even more determined to prove them wrong. Yes, there were moments when I wondered if it was all worth the hassle, but they were fleeting. Anyone who thought I was going to quit obviously did not know the sort of person I am."

Briatore tried to remain open-minded. "He's motivated and this is a big chance for him," Briatore told *Autosport*. "There will be a new Renault engine [for 2001] and we want to be more competitive. With Giancarlo Fisichella and

"THERE IS NO DOUBT IN MY MIND THAT JENSON WILL GO ON TO BE A TRULY GREAT GRAND PRIX DRIVER"

FRANK WILLIAMS

⬇ **Jenson battles hard with David Coulthard's McLaren on a damp track during the 2000 Belgian Grand Prix at Spa-Francorchamps, after hitting Jarno Trulli's Jordan and spinning it out of the race.**

📷 sutton-images.com

Jenson we have a nice combination, two young and ambitious drivers."

Frank Williams added wistfully, "There is no doubt in my mind that Jenson will go on to be a truly great Grand Prix driver. He has astonished the Williams team with his immediate grasp of Formula 1 and the calmness of his approach."

Quizzed on whether Button might have it in him to win races, or even a World Championship with Renault, Briatore was more cautious. "Many people have asked that question,' he said, "but we will not be ready to win the World Championship next year. Races, I do not know. To do that you need to have a car that is on the first or second row [of the grid] at least 60 per cent of the time. In 2001, we will try to be really competitive and win races regularly in 2002."

Making progress in Formula 1 is very like making progress through life in general. You take your chances when the opportunities present themselves. You benefit or suffer setbacks from the judgements and decisions made by others. The real trick is to engineer the situation to be in the right place, with the right team, at the most advantageous moment.

For the moment, however, he had the remainder of the 2000 season to complete. After Hockenheim came Jenson's first visit to the Hungaroring, the tortuous little circuit 20km outside of Budapest that has hosted the Hungarian GP since 1986. Ralf and Jenson qualified fourth and eighth, helped by aerodynamic revisions and an upgraded engine specification. Ralf finished fifth, but a throttle control problem caused Jenson to lose power in the closing stages, dropping him back behind Jarno Trulli's Jordan and Eddie Irvine's Jaguar to post a ninth place finish. "Jenson drove an amazingly good defensive race," said Patrick Head. "Certainly I

think he might have been in the points if he hadn't had that problem."

Then came the Belgian Grand Prix at Spa-Francorchamps, that epic track through the pine forests in the south-east of the country, close to the German border. In qualifying, Jenson was simply scintillating, laying the Williams-BMW into the long corners with a measured precision that reminded Patrick Head of Alain Prost's smooth driving style when he drove for the team in 1993 and won his fourth World Championship.

While Mika Häkkinen's McLaren-Mercedes took pole ahead of Jarno Trulli's Jordan, Button stunned the watching pit lane by edging out Michael Schumacher's Ferrari to place his Williams third on the starting grid. "I am absolutely ecstatic," he said. "I thought I could only outqualify Michael Schumacher if he had gone out or fallen off the track or something."

On the morning of the race heavy rain doused the circuit but it stopped well before the scheduled start time. Still, it was decided that the contest should start behind the safety car as there was still a considerable amount of standing water. At the end of the opening lap the safety car pealed into the pits with Häkkinen 0.8sec ahead of Trulli and Button, and that's how they remained. Mika stretched his advantage all the while, until lap four when Jenson got a bit out of shape under braking for the 'Bus stop' chicane before the pits and Schumacher nipped by into third.

Anxious to make up for his slip, Jenson tucked in behind the Ferrari. As Michael dived inside Trulli at the tight La Source hairpin, he tried to follow but ended up hitting the Jordan and spinning it out of the race. Trulli was not amused. "I think Jenson was a bit too aggressive too soon," he said. "He should have waited for a couple of laps as he would have probably got past me since I was struggling slightly. There was not enough room for Jenson to overtake as well as Schumacher, so he hit me."

After the promise of the opening laps, Button survived to finish a disappointing sixth on a day when Mika Häkkinen brilliantly caught and passed Michael Schumacher's Ferrari to post what many regarded as the greatest victory of his F1 career. Ralf Schumacher was third in the other Williams-BMW, separated from Button by David Coulthard's fourth placed McLaren.

The Italian Grand Prix at Monza rounded off the European season as usual. But the race will be remembered for the multiple pile-up at the second chicane on the opening lap. This triggered a storm of flying debris, a piece of which killed a trackside marshal, 30-year-old Paolo Ghislimberti. With cars scattered in all directions, the safety car was called out to lead the field slowly round while the track was cleared.

← Jenson celebrates after qualifying third at Spa for the 2000 Belgian Grand Prix.
📷 sutton-images.com

⬇ Jenson with BMW Motorsport director Mario Theissen in the pits at Sepang. It was a difficult first year for BMW in partnership with Williams, but Theissen quickly formed a high opinion of Jenson's capability.
📷 LAT

The safety car's flashing lights were turned off on lap 11, signalling to the field that it would be pulling into the pits at the end of that lap. In preparation for the resumption of racing, Schumacher slowed suddenly as he came down towards the right-hand Parabolica turn in an attempt to warm up his brakes and tyres after miles of running at below race speed. The cars in the queue behind braked hard and Jenson, running sixth, suddenly found himself faced with the back of Giancarlo Fisichella's slowing Benetton, and he lurched onto the grass to avoid a collision.

A glancing impact with the barrier damaged his Williams's suspension and he slid off at the next corner, ending up in the gravel trap. Michael later apologised,

but Jenson was not amused. "I am very annoyed," he said. "I got told off for overtaking under the safety car, but I think I avoided quite a big accident. Jacques Villeneuve [a few cars ahead in the queue] stood on the brakes so as not to overtake the people in front, but I had nowhere to go and just missed a marshal standing at the side of the track."

So that was the end of Jenson Button's first Italian Grand Prix. He would also retire from the inaugural US Grand Prix at Indianapolis with an engine failure. But finished a superb fifth in the Japanese Grand Prix at Suzuka after qualifying fifth on the grid, one place ahead of Ralf Schumacher. "My start was quite disastrous," said Jenson. "Having started fifth, I dropped back to seventh but just kept pushing. The car was well balanced and worked very well. I was putting

in quite good times, although obviously not as good as Ferrari or McLaren."

Now he had served his apprenticeship and it was time to leave Williams for the less certain waters of the Renault squad. "Jenson was really the discovery of the year," said Frank Williams. "I don't think anybody would deny that. He was very popular in the team, and both his driving talent and his potential spoke for themselves."

"Jenson was excellent," added Patrick Head. "He probably had a few more engine problems early in the season compared with Ralf, but he was a quick learner and adapted well to the challenge of circuits which were unfamiliar to him. In short, he was almost perfect. Jenson also rattled Ralf's cage and he didn't like it one bit."

[04]

ONWARDS AND UPWARDS

Although Frank Williams had a long-term option on Button's services, he effectively blessed his move to Benetton-Renault in 2001 where he would be partnered by Giancarlo Fisichella. He had a tough time integrating with the team, largely because there had been so much expectation surrounding his efforts the previous year. Now he was just another young driver wrestling with an undeveloped car. His lack of seasoning was about to show, perhaps more than at any time in his career.

Yet Patrick Head certainly knew what Williams was giving up in terms of long-term quality by allowing Button to slip through their fingers at the end of 2000, of that there was no mistake, even though that residual obligation to Montoya meant that their hands were tied.

"We've always thought that Jenson was outstanding and we would have loved to carry on with him," Head said at Monaco in 2009. "He's always had great driving skill. People have likened his style to Alain Prost's in terms of economy of effort, but although it looks very smooth it's actually lots of little movements right on the edge, very controlled. And now he has experience, calmness, judgment and other things. He's also [now] in the right place at the right time, and good luck to him."

Head roundly rejected the criticisms of those who felt that, in the early years, Button was too ready to grab the rewards – the girls, the yacht, the Monaco apartment – before winning the prizes that would justify them. "It's

laughable," Head said. "Tell me which racing driver doesn't like a bit of fun. All the best ones have liked chasing girls and having a good time."

The ethos at Benetton was different to that prevailing within most contemporary F1 teams. In a sense the contrast with Williams couldn't have been greater. Like Williams it was underpinned by solid engineering and an ingrained competitive spirit. But while Williams and Patrick Head were unashamed petrol heads, Benetton's team principal Flavio Briatore was made of very different stuff. Part businessman, part playboy, he'd gained a reputation for working hard and playing harder. Whether it was spending time at his luxury estate in Kenya, lolling on a yacht in the Mediterranean or wandering the pit lane at Monte Carlo, Briatore cut a very different figure to that which the F1 establishment was used to dealing with.

Since entering the Forumla 1 arena in 1989, Briatore had also developed into one of the most astute and influential of all the F1 powerbrokers. In a sense, as he freely admitted, it was because he was not a motorsport fan and could therefore slip the sport's problems into a wider focus than some of his more established colleagues. Flavio was an entrepreneur, a wheeler dealer. He believed that F1 should be glamorous, spectacular and connected with the wider TV-viewing public. He didn't regard it as a niche pastime aimed at the dyed-in-the-wool enthusiast.

"When I first came into Formula 1 in 1989 [as Benetton

← **A new start. For 2001, Jenson changed his colours to those of Benetton-Renault.** LAT

→ **2001 Benetton drivers (from left); Jenson, Giancarlo Fisichella, Fernando Alonso and Mark Webber at the launch of the Benetton B201 in Venice.**
📷 LAT

team principal], it was really a game for engineers," he said. "It was a battle for technology. But it always seemed to me that we were rather missing the point. Here was a huge international show, a global televised event, yet … nobody seemed to be thinking about their public." Briatore had worked on the Milan stock exchange in the early 1970s at a time when the Benetton clothing empire was starting its spectacular growth. In 1979 the Treviso-based company opened its first five stores in the US; three years later Briatore took charge of their marketing operation across the Atlantic.

In 1989 Luciano Benetton asked him to look at their struggling Formula One team. He went to the Australian Grand Prix, looked at it through a shopkeeper's eyes and took the job as team principal.

"I knew nothing at all about Formula One before I came into the sport. But my commercial schooling was with Benetton, a very aggressive company. For us, the product was super important, because we were selling millions of items. But the marketing was also very important as well. But in Formula One, nobody was talking about marketing or lifestyle. Only technology, technology, technology."

If Jenson had any doubts that Briatore was different, he had only to wait for the official launch of the Benetton B201-Renault. It took place in the dramatic surroundings of St Mark's Square in the middle of Venice with hundreds of the world's motorsport media flown in specially for the occasion and transported from Venice airport in a flotilla of chartered cruisers.

"I want Jenson because I believe what he has done this year in his first season has been quite impressive," Flavio told *Autosport*. "I never saw him make any big mistakes in the race or fail to finish because of his own error, even though he has been racing on some circuits that he did not know before. And if you look at how he went at Silverstone, which he knew well, he was very quick. I think the guy is good. I hope we can give him a competitive car and we'll see what happens. He's young and nice for Formula One. He's good with the sponsors and the public. He needs to be more aggressive, but that is part of experience."

Renault's purchase of the Benetton team at the start of the 2000 season was part of a long-term project to mesh the French car maker's pedigree as a leading-edge F1 engine specialist with Benetton's high-tech chassis capability. In 2000, the team had used a Supertec V10, derived from the engine used in Jacques Villeneuve's 1997 World Championship-winning Williams. But for 2001 the team switched to an all-new 111° V10 developed by Jean-Jacques His and his team at Renault Sport.

It would prove to be a disappointing season for Jenson. His team-mate Giancarlo Fisichella would outqualify him 13–4 over the course of the year and looked a more convincing operator than the young British driver. "In my view, Fisichella was quicker than Jenson's previous team-mate Ralf Schumacher at Williams," said Mike Gascoyne, Renault's technical director, "and that made it difficult for him and he had to work hard to adapt. He knuckled down in the second half of the year and got his head down much better once we had a two-car test team up and running."

As usual, the 2001 season opened with the Australian Grand Prix at Melbourne's splendid Albert Park circuit. Twelve months after all the media interest surrounding Jenson's debut for Williams, the attention switched to his successor, the Indy 500 winner Juan Pablo Montoya. In the Benetton camp, life looked stressful and difficult. On the morning of qualifying, Jenson's car needed a gearbox change while Fisichella's B201 developed a water leak. They qualified 16th and 17th, well off the pace.

Come the race, things could hardly have gone worse for Jenson. He incurred a 10-second stop–go penalty after the stewards judged that his mechanics had remained too long on the starting grid prior to the formation lap. Later in the race, with just six laps to go, a broken exhaust caused the wiring loom to burn through, and forced Jenson to retire. He withdrew from the contest almost unnoticed.

It was difficult to know where to look for reassurance. In Malaysia they were 16th and 17th on the grid, both drivers struggling for grip and handling balance, but this time Fisichella was fractionally ahead. In the race, Jenson was once again little more than a footnote, trailing home 11th. It was difficult to see how it could get any worse. But in Brazil, on the Autodromo Jose Carlos Pace at Interlagos, that's precisely what happened. Beset by oil leaks and a generally dismal performance Fisichella lined up 18th, two places ahead of Button. Button finished 10th, three laps behind David Coulthard's victorious McLaren Mercedes.

But there was nothing they could do in the short-term. Drastic technical compromises were being forced on the team because the new Renault V10 was around 100bhp down on its rivals. It was no joke trying to race the opposition in such circumstances. There were cylinder block problems to be surmounted, but nothing in Formula One can be changed overnight. Major engineering problems take time. It began to look like Button's career was being wrecked on the rocks of Benetton's lack of competitiveness.

"We always knew that the first part of the season would be a problem," said Gascoyne. "It would have been all-too-easy to have opted for another season with the old Supertec V10 and we might well have ended up as high as

⬇ **A blaze of colour as Jenson pushes during Friday practice for the 2001 Brazilian Grand Prix at Interlagos.**
📷 LAT

season, the San Marino Grand Prix at Imola's Autodromo Enzo e Dino Ferrari. No chance. Jenson crept onto the back of the grid with the 21st fastest time and shared the final row with Tarso Marques in the Minardi. The race turned out to be another one to forget.

On lap 19 Jenson brought the Benetton B201 into the pits from 17th place for what turned out to be a 7.4-second refuelling stop. Unfortunately, a malfunction with the refuelling rig meant that no fuel went into the car and he had to come in again next time around, which dropped him down close to last. Eventually Jenson struggled home in 12th, hampered by his earlier refuelling difficulties and experiencing shoulder strain.

Briatore attempted to put an optimistic gloss on the situation. "At the moment we are just attempting to survive, but from the French Grand Prix onwards we hope to be upping the power and closing the performance gap," he said. It sounded like a forlorn hope.

Jenson finished 15th in the Spanish Grand Prix at Barcelona, a truly dreadful showing. He had another oil leak during practice for the Austrian Grand Prix at the A1-Ring, then trailed around at the back in the race after again qualifying on the back row with Tarso Marques. He eventually spun off on his own oil after his engine expired. Thankfully, things improved a touch for Jenson's second visit to Monaco. Mike Gascoyne predicted that the B201's low-speed performance on a track where aerodynamic grip was less of an issue, would give the team a boost.

This certainly proved the case for Fisichella who managed to qualify an excellent tenth. Button was 17th, but come the race their fortunes reversed. 'Fisi' survived one brush with the unyielding guard rail, but came a cropper for a second time and retired from the race with damaged suspension. Jenson finished a solid seventh, lapped by Michael Schumacher's winning Ferrari. He was 28 seconds away from scoring his first championship point

fifth in the World Championship rankings. But the trouble is that we'd have faced the prospect of tackling 2002 in the knowledge that we had little realistic prospect of finishing better than fifth in that year's championship either.

"We had no alternative but to press on as boldly as we could. We had to accept compromises at the start of the season in the hope that we could make progress at the other end of the year. Sure, as racers, it was very frustrating to turn up to those early season races knowing we were going to qualify 18th or 19th. But we really didn't want to waste time on short-term fixes."

The Benetton top brass might have hoped things would take a turn for the better at the first European race of the

> ## "WE HAD NO ALTERNATIVE BUT TO PRESS ON AS BOLDLY AS WE COULD. WE HAD TO ACCEPT COMPROMISES AT THE START OF THE SEASON IN THE HOPE THAT WE COULD MAKE PROGRESS AT THE OTHER END OF THE YEAR"
>
> ### MIKE GASCOYNE

at the wheel of a Benetton, that being the distance he trailed Jean Alesi's Prost-Ferrari at the chequered flag.

At the Canadian Grand Prix in Montréal, Benetton should have had both cars equipped with power steering for the first time, but the systems were not ready in time. Jenson at least managed to lift himself off the back row of the grid, but 20th wasn't anything to write home about and after 17 laps he pulled off when his car developed an oil leak. The European Grand Prix at the Nürburgring produced little consolation either. "Understeer and no grip," shrugged Button after another disappointing 20th place on the grid. He trailed home 13th, two laps behind Schumacher's victorious Ferrari. The nightmare seemed endless, with precious little in terms of light to be seen flickering at the end of the tunnel.

Finally, at the French Grand Prix, there was some hope in Renault's back yard. They fitted a revised aerodynamic package to the cars as well as a new specification Renault engine, which both drivers judged to be a definite step in the right direction. Fisichella qualified 16th, Jenson 17th, but Button admitted that he hadn't really done himself justice even allowing for the fact that his first run was spoiled by Eddie Irvine's Jaguar spinning in front of him. "My second run was better," he said, "but I'm afraid I mucked up the next two because I was supposed to adjust the differential setting after the second corner. Unfortunately, I forgot to do so on both occasions."

Again, another wretched race ensued for the Benetton team-mates. Fisichella touched Jos Verstappen's Arrows

↑ **Jenson kept the Benetton out of the barriers in Monaco to net seventh place in this most exacting of Grand Prix races.**
📷 LAT

↑ **Visiting the Springfield Boys' Club for underprivileged youngsters in London.**
📷 LAT

↓ **Battling with Pedro de la Rosa during the opening lap of the 2001 Belgian Grand Prix.**
📷 LAT

at the start, and lost a few places in the process. Giancarlo judged that must have done some minor damage as the car felt odder and odder under hard braking as the race progressed. That said, the Italian's day was a whole lot better than Button's whose afternoon ended with a spin into a gravel trap after 68 laps, probably due to engine failure. He was classified 16th, four laps down on the winning Ferrari. "The engine started to cut out before my second refuelling stop and when I pitted Giancarlo was already there," said Button. "Not ideal, but because I had a fuel pressure problem and had no option but to come in at that moment."

In terms of pure track performance, Jenson's second British Grand Prix passed with more of a whimper than a bang. As Mika Häkkinen surged to victory for McLaren-Mercedes, Jenson struggled round at the back of the field in his now customary position, creeping past the chequered flag in 15th, again two laps down on the winner. In terms of pit lane credibility, Button had dropped from the radar screen. Formula One is an unforgiving business – you are only as good as your last race, nothing more nor less. The fact that the Benetton B201 was a pretty average

piece of equipment at best was almost irrelevant. The truth of the matter was that Fisichella was overshadowing Button in the same car, and that simply wasn't good for the English driver's CV.

At Hockenheim, Fisichella and Button lined up 17th and 18th on the grid for the German Grand Prix after showing precious little in the way of the promise they would unlock for the race. A multiple first corner accident, which saw Luciano Burti's Prost vaulting over Michael Schumacher's Ferrari, and leaving the track surface coated with razor-sharp shards of carbon-fibre, resulted in the race being red flagged to a halt. After the restart the punishing nature of the circuit, allied with 30°C-plus temperatures, exacted a high toll in terms of mechanical unreliability. Yet on this occasion the two Benettons proved to be bulletproof, touring home fourth and fifth to claim a double helping of World Championship points.

"I drove conservatively in the early stages," said Fisichella, "and saved enough fuel to do a slightly longer first stint than planned. When I rejoined, I was ahead of Jenson and things continued to go well, although I ran slightly wide near the end and lost a bit of time." For his part Button was quick to make the point that the Benettons were hardly makeweights in this particular race. "My car was very well balanced and I think we were quicker than the Jordans and BARs when we were running the same fuel load," he said. "But I had one problem. I pulled my water bottle tube out of my mouth so it was spraying all over my face whenever I braked. It wasn't an easy race, especially with Alesi right behind, but it was good fun."

Yet the German Grand Prix would only give the Benetton drivers' morale a momentary uplift. In Hungary, Button qualified 17th, collected a 10-second stop–go penalty for an accidental jump start, then spun off the road after 34 laps while running at the tail of the field. Then at Spa-Francorchamps further aerodynamic improvements and another engine upgrade saw Fisichella and Button qualifying sixth and tenth. Giancarlo had demonstrated the effectiveness of the team's launch control system by hurtling down the outside at the start to tuck immediately into second place behind Michael Schumacher's Ferrari.

By the end of the opening lap Fisichella was still hanging on just 3.7 seconds behind Michael, with Rubens Barrichello third in the other Ferrari, and the McLaren-Mercedes of David Coulthard and Mika Häkkinen sandwiching Jenson's Benetton, which was holding fifth place. He was still running fifth on lap 18 when he hit one of the rubber cones delineating the left-hand kerb on the entry to the so-called 'Bus Stop' chicane just before the start line. He skittered on straight into the wall as the front wing of his Benetton was pulled off. It tucked under the left front wheel, momentarily jamming up the steering.

A fortnight later it looked as though Jenson was about to make up for this slip when he qualified 11th for the Italian Grand Prix at Monza. This was a tense event run

↑ **Jenson looks pensive prior to qualifying for the 2001 British Grand Prix at Silverstone. He qualified a disappointing 18th and finished the race in 15th place, two laps behind winner Mika Häkkinen.**
📷 LAT

under the emotional cloud of the 9/11 terrorist outrage in New York which had taken place the previous week. There were signs of mourning all over the paddock. The Ferraris ran devoid of any sponsorship identification and with black nose cones. The Jaguar airboxes similarly were dressed in black. The Jordans carried the stars and stripes on their airboxes out of respect. Then, on Saturday, the dreadful news filtered through to the track that Alex Zanardi, the popular Italian driver who Button had replaced in the Williams team the previous year, had lost both his legs in a terrible accident during a CART race at the Lausitzring oval circuit near Dresden.

For the jangled, tautly stretched nerves in the Monza paddock, this somehow seemed the last straw on the eve

of the Grand Prix. The Schumacher brothers tried to rally support for a 'no passing' deal until the first two chicanes on the opening lap of the race had been negotiated. This didn't come to anything. Then it was suggested that the race might be started behind the safety car, but that was vetoed by Briatore, BAR boss Craig Pollock and Arrows boss Tom Walkinshaw. They all insisted that their drivers should just get on and do their jobs. "Briatore is a bully and this is a disgrace," fumed Jean Alesi.

The race duly went ahead as tempers calmed, but it was to prove a bad day for Button who accidentally slammed into the back of Jarno Trulli's Jordan while braking into the first corner. Trulli was furious. "Button hit the rear of my car as he turned in and pushed me into a spin," he said. "He

Finally came Suzuka, and the Japanese Grand Prix, the traditional upbeat finale to the F1 season. Fisichella demonstrated just how formidable Renault's qualifying-spec V10 had become by bagging sixth on the grid, three places ahead of Button. Jenson finished seventh, just missing out on a championship point. But he was on the same lap as Michael Schumacher's victorious Ferrari at the chequered flag, which reflected the progress Benetton had made.

The bottom line for Jenson was 17th place in the World Championship stakes with just those two points from the fifth place at Hockenheim to his credit. His best grid position had been ninth; his worst 21st. He'd now completed 34 Formula One races during which he'd accumulated 14 championship points. Compared with that glorious maiden season with Williams, it all looked rather disappointing. But the upside was that Jenson was adding to his experience. The first season at Benetton had made him tougher, more reslient. Now he had to build on that experience in a bid to make more sense of things in 2002.

Fisichella left for 2002 and Button found himself partnering Jarno Trulli in the Renault squad. Button began to pick up the pace now with excellent fourth places in both Malaysia and Brazil, only losing what would have been his first podium finish at Sepang when he was overtaken by Michael Schumacher on the final lap. Yet now he had to face up to another challenge. Flavio Briatore had decided to replace him for 2003 with his young protégé Fernando Alonso. Jenson had to look for another team.

For the 2002 season, the team's cars were now officially identified as Renault R202s, the Benetton branding now put firmly behind them. As it turned out, the team would end up fourth in the Constructors' Championship, although the 23 points scored by Button and his new team-mate Jarno Trulli would be collected in dribs and drabs, neither man scoring a single podium finish during the course of the season.

← Jenson loses his front wing after hitting the back of Jarno Trulli's Jordan while braking into the first corner at Monza in the 2001 Italian Grand Prix.
📷 LAT

↓ The Benettons featured a 'Stars and Stripes' flag for the 2001 US Grand Prix at Indianapolis, as a mark of respect for those who lost their lives in the 9/11 terrorist outrage in New York earlier in the month.
📷 sutton-images.com

clearly badly misjudged his braking but I was already in the corner, so there was nothing I could do."

"I braked at the same time as everybody else," Jenson apologised, "but I couldn't stop in time to avoid Trulli. I ran into the back of him, lost my front wing and put him out of the race, for which I was very sorry." Jenson pitted for repairs, but engine failure claimed him three laps later.

The US Grand Prix at Indianapolis brought better fortune for the Renault squad with Jenson qualifying well with the tenth fastest time, two places ahead of Fisichella. "It's great to be in the top ten for the first time this year," he said. "I just hope this time we can do something at the start and make it round!" He finished ninth, just behind Fisichella, but a lap behind Mika Häkkinen's victorious McLaren.

The year started with Renault Sport chairman Patrick Faure confirming that the team would be extremely disappointed if it failed to end up fourth in the championship. The technical programme was again presided over by Mike Gascoyne as technical director and the vastly experienced Pat Symonds in the role of director of engineering. The R202 was powered by a refined version of the wide 111° V10 engine and the management very clearly set out its stall with Gascoyne stating that it was Renault's intention "to win the championship in 2005 and beyond."

Trulli, joining the Renault squad after a somewhat bruising spell with Jordan, performed more conservatively in the opening races of the year. It was almost as if he felt he had to take things easy, that easing himself progressively into the routine of a front-line team was the best way in which to recalibrate his own personal performance. That, in part, contributed to Button being the quicker performer in the first half of the year. Later, however, when he knew he would be leaving the team, Button's form would fade slightly. "Disappointing, but understandable," said Gascoyne sympathetically.

⬇ **Keeping fit in style. The Renault F1 squad, Jenson, Fernando Alonso and Jarno Trulli, training in Kenya just before Christmas 2001.**
📷 Renault F1

Of course, this was another example of just how difficult it is to get a driver's ultimate potential into correct focus on the shifting sands of F1's ever-changing fortune. Objectively, one must conclude that the 2002 Renault was probably not as good as its strongest proponents claimed, and in fact Button was much better than the equipment allowed him to look.

Yet he was, to a large extent, swept along on a flood tide of events. There was always the lingering suspicion that, for all the kindly words of encouragement, Briatore did not really have the faith in him that he professed he did.

Truth be told, 2002 was an awkward balancing act for Jenson. He showed just enough form to be rated as 'good enough', but you had to understand the F1 business, and have the inclination to scratch the surface of events, to really appreciate that Button had potential far beyond the results he had delivered so far.

Ferrari, of course, remained the F1 pace setters in 2002. So confident in their own potential, the Maranello brigade arrived in Melbourne for the opening race of the year without bothering to bring their new F2002 challenger. They correctly judged that Michael Schumacher and

← Trouble ahead. Fernando Alonso, Renault's new test driver, poses between Trulli and Button at the start of the 2002 season. Mid-season the Spaniard would be confirmed as Jenson's replacement for the following year.
📷 LAT

Rubens Barrichello could still get the job done at this early stage of the season with the previous year's title-winning F2001. Their prime challengers were Kimi Räikkönen and David Coulthard in the new McLaren MP4/17Ds plus Ralf Schumacher and Juan Pablo Montoya in their Williams FW24s. Realistically, the Renault duo could be regarded as 'best of the rest'.

Jenson qualified 11th, four places behind Trulli, but he celebrated the start of his second season with the Briatore brigade by failing to get beyond the first corner of the race. Accelerating away from pole position, Barrichello's Ferrari was hit from behind by Ralf Schumacher's Williams-BMW. As Ralf's car reared up over the back of the Italian machine it looked for a heart-stopping moment as if it might execute a backward flip. Thankfully the Williams came crashing back down on its wheels and skidded off into the gravel trap at the first turn. In its wake there was mayhem as the pack scattered in all directions.

Jenson was one of the casualties whose race ended there and then. Others out on the spot included Allan McNish's Toyota, Olivier Panis's BAR-Honda, the Saubers of Nick Heidfeld and Felipe Massa, and Giancarlo Fisichella's Jordan. All in all, it was a pretty bad day at the office.

A very different outcome awaited Button in the sweltering heat of Malaysia a fortnight later. There Jenson reported himself quite happy with the handling of his R202, posting an eighth fastest time on his first run. After that he had a slight engine problem and switched to the spare car, which he felt was just as good. By contrast, Trulli wound up a disappointed 12th, unhappy with the balance of his car.

Button ran strongly from the start, avoiding the first corner collision between Schumacher's Ferrari and Montoya's Williams, which left Michael trailing into the pits for a replacement nose section to be fitted and Montoya back in 11th. He would be further delayed by the imposition of a drive-through penalty for causing the unscheduled brush between the two cars. Michael rejoined 19th, some 45 seconds behind the leaders and proceeded

"OBVIOUSLY I'M DISAPPOINTED NOT TO HAVE GOT MY FIRST PODIUM, BUT I FELT A PROBLEM WITH THE SUSPENSION TWO LAPS FROM THE END AND THE CAR BEGAN RUNNING ON THREE WHEELS"

JENSON BUTTON

↑ **A busy pit-stop during the 2002 Malaysian Grand Prix at Sepang. Jenson was set for a podium finish when a rear suspension problem in the closing stages allowed Michael Schumacher to pass him for third.**

📷 LAT

to drive absolutely flat-out with all the determination and motivation of a first-year F1 novice.

In the closing stages it looked as though Ralf Schumacher, who'd driven a perfect race and kept out of trouble on a two-stop strategy, would lead Montoya home for a Williams 1–2 with the team's old boy Jenson joining them on the rostrum. But there was a sting in the race's tail yet to come, much to Button's acute disappointment.

After driving what many people regarded as the finest race of his career, the Renault's rear suspension developed a problem in the closing stages of the race after a tie-rod broke and Michael's Ferrari slipped by on the final lap. "It was an excellent race for me in spite of the

problem at the end," he said. "Obviously I'm disappointed not to have got my first podium, but I felt a problem with the suspension two laps from the end and the car began running on three wheels."

Disappointed though he may have been, Malaysia signalled that the new Renault was a competitive proposition. For the Brazilian Grand Prix at Interlagos, Trulli and Button qualified sixth and seventh after an excellent effort, then vaulted ahead of the two McLarens to run third and fourth behind Michael and Ralf Schumacher by the end of the opening lap. Barrichello soon stormed through to second, but the Renaults kept in touch with both McLarens for much of the race, eventually leapfrogging them by virtue of staying out longer for their sole refuelling stop. In the end, Trulli's dismal luck continued when his engine blew while in fifth place 11 laps from the end. That promoted Jenson to his place after which he received a late race bonus when Räikkönen's right rear wheel hub failed four laps from the chequered flag and the Finn's McLaren pirouetted into retirement.

As he settled into his business class seat for the 14-hour flight back to Europe, Jenson could have been forgiven for permitting himself a wry grin. With three of the season's races completed he was holding fourth place in the Drivers' Championship, admittedly with a modest six points that looked pretty slim when compared with Michael Schumacher's 24. He consolidated his position in the rankings with a respectable fifth place in the San Marino GP at Imola. But at the Spanish Grand Prix an even more promising result was snatched away by hydraulic failure after he'd qualified sixth and run as high as third at one point.

At the Circuit de Catalunya, Button was driving superbly. On the face of it this was quite a turn around, with Coulthard chasing the Renault for all he was worth in the opening phase. He duly gained time on Button through the

first spate of refuelling stops and eventually outbraked him neatly into the right-hander beyond the pits at the start of lap 34. Disappointingly, thereafter Jenson found the car getting progressively more difficult to drive and Trulli nipped past only a couple of laps later.

"The car wasn't fantastic at the beginning of the race

⬆**A humorous message of encouragement for Jenson from his loyal fans.**
📷 sutton-images.com

⬅**Jenson stretching the legs of the new Renault R202 on his way to a brilliant fourth in the 2002 Brazilian Grand Prix at Interlagos. He started seventh on the grid.**
📷 LAT

with high-speed understeer and oversteer in the slower corners," he said. "We didn't manage to adjust the car to correct this during the pit stops and then I had an hydraulic problem. The steering got very heavy and it was as if somebody had switched the electrics off towards the end." With Coulthard finishing third behind Schumacher's Ferrari and Montoya's Williams, Jenson now found himself demoted to fifth place in the points table.

Of course, in theatrical terms, Renault were bit-part players on the F1 scene and that reality was to be dramatically underlined in the Austrian Grand Prix. The race ended with Rubens Barrichello handing Michael Schumacher victory on the final corner, just as he'd given second place to him behind David Coulthard's McLaren 12 months earlier. This heavy-handed performance from Ferrari hardly endeared the Prancing Horse to the army of race fans in the grandstands, nor indeed to the FIA, which called the team's management to account at the next

been unsettling to have Briatore's nominee effectively sizing up the cockpit of his car even before the 2002 season reached the halfway mark.

Alonso was clearly something of a prodigy. Winner of the Spa F3000 race in 2000 when he was 19 years old, he had driven the uncompetitive Minardi with flashes of genius the following year. Sitting in the Monaco media centre, my colleague Nigel Roebuck suddenly commented, "Who the hell is *that*?" We looked up to see an in-car cockpit shot of somebody working away with lightning reactions and razor-sharp precision. It was Alonso on a qualifying lap. Now he was bounding around the pits in a Renault shirt, keeping a watchful eye on Button.

Jenson qualified an excellent eighth on his third Formula One outing at Monaco, one place behind his team-mate. But in the race everything went wrong. He crept slightly on the grid, anticipating the start by a fraction of a second, for which transgression he was awarded a drive-through

"I COULD SEE THAT PANIS WAS STRUGGLING WITH HIS REAR TYRES AND TRIED TO PASS HIM AT STE DEVOTE. HE DIDN'T SEE ME AND JUST TOOK HIS NORMAL LINE"

JENSON BUTTON

meeting of the World Motorsport Council. None of this really concerned Jenson who finished a decent seventh, the only Renault to finish after Trulli succumbed to fuel pressure problems.

Jenson seemed to be getting on well in the Renault camp. But was he? By the time the teams rolled into Monte Carlo for their customary annual binge with the billionaire brigade, there were some pit lane observers who smelt trouble in the air. Rumour had it that John Byfield's preliminary talks about extending Jenson's contract with Renault had run up against something of a brick wall in the shape of Flavio Briatore. The enigmatic Italian entrepreneur's FBB management company had a stake in Trulli's future, but he was less interested in Button. That was largely because he'd taken the young Spanish driver Fernando Alonso under his commercial wing a couple of years earlier, helped place him at Minardi for 2001 and later signed him as Renault's test driver. Although Button never showed any indication that he was uneasy, it must have

penalty. Overtaking in contemporary F1 is difficult enough in normal circumstances, let alone trying to climb back through the field in Monte Carlo from a lowly position near the back of the pack. He survived until lap 52 when he got a little too ambitious trying to overtake Olivier Panis's BAR-Honda at Ste Devote and the two cars rattled into the barriers.

"I think I just got a little excited at the start," said Jenson. "After that I was a bit surprised to be penalised as well, but once I got the car into clear air it was working well. As for the accident, I could see that Panis was struggling with his rear tyres and tried to pass him at Ste Devote. He didn't see me and just took his normal line."

In Canada Button's car overheated into retirement but at the European Grand Prix at the Nürburgring he came home a heartening fifth, although by then he was down in seventh place in the Drivers' Championship with 10 points; Michael Schumacher had 76. Two weeks later he had an undistinguished run in the British Grand Prix from

→ **Jenson chats to his future boss Ross Brawn during a function at the 2002 Goodwood Festival of Speed.**
📷 Getty Images

↓ **Sandwiched between Kimi Räikkönen's McLaren and team-mate Jarno Trulli's Renault during the 2002 European Grand Prix at Nürburgring. Jenson finished an excellent fifth.**
📷 LAT

which he retired with a loose front wheel with six laps to go. Things were not looking too promising now.

Meanwhile, behind the scenes contractual negotiations were in full flow. Briatore had decided that Alonso would drive for Renault in 2003. The decision was confirmed on the Saturday afternoon at the French Grand Prix. Suddenly Jenson looked ever-so-slightly beleaguered, enveloped in a fog of media speculation. What would he do now? Go to Jaguar perhaps to replace Eddie Irvine? No, it would be the BAR-Honda squad. Even before the French Grand Prix had begun, the team's PR staff were passing round invitations to a press conference in London the day after the race. Jenson and David Richards had signed on the dotted line, guaranteeing Button a long-term contract with the team that the millionaire rallying entrepreneur was absolutely determined to transform into a winning proposition.

It still looked something of a risk, but Richards was supremely confident. "When you build a block of flats, or an office, first you dig a hole in the ground and you follow that with substantial foundations," he said. "It may take a year, perhaps longer, before it becomes obvious

what you are doing, before the building rises above the ground, but all that time you are working away behind the scenes preparing for the future. That's what it was like at BAR during the summer of 2002. We knew where we intended to go, but it wasn't always easy to persuade people that we might get there in the end. But we were certainly working towards that aim."

Button was to replace Olivier Panis in the BAR squad as the Frenchman had accepted an invitation to switch to the Toyota team. Olivier would be a hard act for Jenson to follow. Not only was he a highly popular, charismatic personality, but he'd arrived at BAR with a well merited reputation as a test and development driver. That reputation was built up with McLaren, where both David Coulthard and Mika Häkkinen had developed total faith in his conclusions about the cars he'd been driving. He was also very quick and his convivial nature ensured that he got on well with Jacques Villeneuve, the sometimes temperamental former champion who was still very much a central character in the BAR-Honda story.

Villeneuve's response to the news of Button's impending arrival was so matter-of-fact as to border on the totally disinterested. "I guess he will bring youth to the team," he said dismissively. "But not experience, as he hasn't got much. Last year [2001] was a season lost for him, but this year he has overshadowed Trulli and has been doing a good job. We get along. That is very important, because it is never enjoyable to be around someone you don't like." On reflection, the implications of Villeneuve's comments were curious. Button was coming into the BAR-Honda squad with three years' experience as a Grand Prix driver under his belt. He was therefore hardly inexperienced. Yet perhaps Villeneuve was being very shrewd by not identifying Button as a serious rival. Perhaps he wanted to keep him guessing as to what his real feelings were. It was difficult to say, but then Jacques had always been a very difficult person to read.

The net result of all this activity was that Button entered that strange limbo land occupied by drivers who are seeing out their contract with one team in the knowledge that arrangements are already in place for them to move to another team the following year. No matter how hard you try to avoid the situation, there is inevitably a perceptible cooling of the relationship. So it was with Renault and Button. Their interest in him seemed to cool ever so slightly, fuelled in part by the fact that Alonso was already testing regularly for the team. In their mind he was the next Big Thing. Jenson was yesterday's news. Yet for all that, there remained a certain respect for the young British driver and Mike Gascoyne

later commented on several occasions that his personal biggest disappointment in 2002 was Button's failure to finish on the podium in Malaysia after such a superb drive.

Button finished sixth in the French Grand Prix, but when he arrived at Hockenheim, the newly truncated track near Heidelberg which played host to the German Grand Prix, he found himself battling against the tide. He lost half the Saturday free practice session due to an engine failure, which effectively left him desperately attempting to regain lost ground. "I then made a couple of mistakes on my qualifying run which meant that I couldn't improve on 13th," he said. In the race he retired after 24 laps with transmission problems.

In Hungary Button spun off and in the Belgian Grand Prix at Spa-Francorchamps he suffered an engine failure ten

↑ Jenson looks thoughtful at the French Grand Prix in April 2002 after learning that he would be dropped from the Renault F1 team at the end of the year.
◉ LAT

laps into the 44-lap event. Things went better at Monza, although having to start in 17th place after a spin into a gravel trap didn't look too promising by the end of Saturday afternoon. Come the race, things proved much better. He and Trulli both did a great job, the two Renault drivers opting for one-stop refuelling strategies with a short opening stint, which carried them through to fourth and fifth places at the finish.

"I thought I'd lost everything at the start," said Trulli. "First gear didn't engage properly when I went through the launch control process, so I had to start from the back of the grid. After that, finishing fourth was pretty unexpected. Mika Salo's Toyota held us both up during the early stages of the race, so we decided to modify our strategy and make our pit stop earlier than planned." At the flag, Jarno was just 6 seconds behind Eddie Irvine's Jaguar.

Just two races were left now in Jenson's Renault career. He finished eighth in the US Grand Prix in Indianapolis and had a moderately satisfying finale at Suzuka where sixth in the Japanese race left him seventh in the championship on 14 points, one place ahead of team-mate Jarno Trulli on nine points. Michael Schumacher had more than ten times Jenson's tally, with 144 points to his credit.

At the end of the 2002 season Jenson rated ninth in the Top Ten driver ratings in the long-established *Autocourse* annual. They concluded, "Button has proved himself a capable performer, yet there are still those who feel he is not sufficiently assertive when it comes to wheel-to-wheel scrapping. He is stylish and sympathetic with the machinery, shows a willingess to learn and is fundamentally very quick. Yet even though he is only 22, he has reached the end of his third season in Formula One without the benefit of the equipment needed to make a decisive mark on the record books. David Richards has said that he believes Button is capable of winning a world championship. This sounds like a prediction made in the euphoria of the moment at the time he secured the services of the young British driver. Whether or not Button can deliver on Richards's promise will depend almost entirely on whether BAR can genuinely transform itself from a shambolic also-ran to the status of a genuine front-line contender."

One thing seemed clear. For all his efforts to become part of the Renault family, Button seemed to have a slightly semi-detached relationship with Briatore's squad. Now at BAR he would find himself working for a team that wanted him unconditionally. The transformation would come. Not immediately. But things were set to get a lot better for Jenson Button's unfolding career prospects.

↑ **Posing for the cameras with new boss David Richards in July 2002 after signing as a BAR-Honda driver for 2003.**
📷 sutton-images.com

→ **Jenson's 'Blue World' was about to change to the white of BAR-Honda.**
📷 LAT

"I GUESS HE WILL BRING YOUTH TO THE TEAM. BUT NOT EXPERIENCE, AS HE HASN'T GOT MUCH… WE GET ALONG. THAT IS VERY IMPORTANT, BECAUSE IT IS NEVER ENJOYABLE TO BE AROUND SOMEONE YOU DON'T LIKE"

JACQUES VILLENEUVE

↑ Jenson climbs from his car after spinning out of the 2002 Hungarian Grand Prix.

sutton-images.com

[05]

GETTING INTO HIS STRIDE

Relationships between team principals and their drivers are crucial to achieving Grand Prix success. While the driver will be looking for the ultimate performance, for all their outward toughness, the truth is that at this level they can display unexpected mental fragility. They need to get on with their employers and feel that those individuals are doing more than simply delivering their pay cheques.

You could see it in Nigel Mansell as he matured under the Williams team's tutelage in 1985. This wasn't a case of Williams producing a sympathetic arm around the shoulder. It was more a matter of giving him a positive environment in which he could unlock his talent. Button was the beneficiary of a similar set-up when he joined Williams in 2000. There was never any doubt in his mind that Frank and Patrick Head played straight with him. From the outset, he knew that Juan Pablo Montoya was lurking in the background as a likely successor in 2001. But Williams never made any secret of that obligation.

"Jenson will have to perform absolutely outstandingly if he is to keep Juan Pablo out of the team next season," said Frank. So Button knew exactly where he was. The situation was less clear-cut during his time at Renault. The team principal Flavio Briatore was always a shrewd operator. When he took on Button in 2001 he seemed enthusiastic enough, outwardly at least. But paddock insiders never thought he displayed the burning confidence in the young

British driver that was reflected by Frank and Patrick. He seemed a touch lukewarm.

From the start of 2002 it didn't look as though Button would have any long-term future at Renault, and so it proved. Briatore's protégé Fernando Alonso, a young Spaniard who had showed terrific natural car control in the tail-end Minardi the previous season, had been taken on to the Renault team as test driver.

The axe fell at the French Grand Prix. On the day before the race, Alonso was confirmed as Button's successor for 2003. Two days later BAR team principal David Richards moved quickly to reveal that he had signed Jenson on a four-year contract, initially as Jacques Villeneuve's partner for the 2003 season. His salary would reputedly be around £3.5 million.

"I was staggered when I heard that Renault were releasing Jenson," said Richards, "and when I was made aware there was no binding issue between him and Williams, I immediately set about securing him. It happened quite quickly, but when you get an opportunity like this you don't sit on the sidelines. You make a quick decision. It's a two-year contract with a two-year option, but I look on it as a four-year contract as that's what it's going to be at the end of the day. And in that period I'm convinced that Jenson is going to be World Champion."

For his part, Button was extremely grateful for the chance with BAR, even though there was the slim

New team, new livery; Jenson is a BAR-Honda man at the start of 2003.
LAT

possibility that he might be tempted with a deal at Jaguar as Eddie Irvine was on schedule to leave at the end of the year if the team didn't renew his £5 million a year contract. Even so, Button was slightly taken aback when Briatore told him he would be out.

"Even though Renault was only an option," he said, "I was slightly shocked as it's been a good, positive season. I had a lot of teams I was talking to about where I wanted to go next year. I've been flattered by the enormous attention I've received as I've had a whole range of opportunities open to me. But one reason I've come here is because of David and what he has done with the team in the past six months. It's a team which will keep on improving."

> "...ONE REASON I'VE COME HERE IS BECAUSE OF DAVID AND WHAT HE HAS DONE WITH THE TEAM IN THE PAST SIX MONTHS. IT'S A TEAM WHICH WILL KEEP ON IMPROVING"
>
> **JENSON BUTTON**

On the face of it this seemd like wild speculation, the sort of prediction made on the spur of the moment. But there was one key issue, absolutely fundamental to the whole package, on which any future success depended. As *Autocourse* noted at the end of 2002: "Whether Button can deliver on Richards' promise will depend almost entirely on whether BAR can transform itself from a shambolic also-ran to the status of genuine front-line contender."

Even in the summer of 2002, the BAR-Honda team was regarded as a bad joke in F1 circles. Conceived by Jacques Villeneuve's personal manager Craig Pollock as a vehicle to sustain the Canadian driver's career after he left Williams at the end of 1998, the project was bankrolled by the giant British American Tobacco concern. Here was a bunch of ambitious young entrepreneurs setting out to overturn the Formula One establishment. They were well-funded, they would operate from a new state-of-the-art factory at Brackley, near Silverstone, and they had the 1997 World Champion on their books as number one driver.

Yet as soon as the BAR-Supertec 001 rolled out onto the circuit at the 1999 Australian Grand Prix, dark clouds began to roll across Pollock's ambition. They finished the first season without scoring a single championship point. The car's performance had been inconsistent and unreliable. Even so, Honda came aboard in 2000 as their engine supply partner. But the only thing BAR proved itself good at was consuming money, oodles of it, an estimated £500 million in its first three years. By the middle of 2001 Honda was at its wit's end with the team's management. They contacted BAT and made it quite clear that if a new regime was not put into place instead of Pollock, then they would be withdrawing from the partnership at the end of that season.

BAT agreed. The only other alternative was to cut their losses, scrap the whole programme and sell the team. That would have meant writing off what most people in the F1 paddock felt had been a singularly ill-judged investment in the first place.

BAT turned to David Richards to help dig them out of this pit of despair. They knew him well and trusted his judgement. Richards was steeped in motorsports know-how. He'd started out as a rally co-driver and won the 1981 World Rally Championship with Ari Vatanen in a semi-works Ford Escort. Then he'd retired and established his own specialist preparation company, eventually called 'Prodrive', which operated from a distinctive landmark base adjacent to the M40 motorway at Banbury. Prodrive's low, white-painted factory was as much its calling card as the company's expertise across the motorsports spectrum.

David's success and business skills led to a pivotal meeting with Fuji Heavy Industries at the Safari Rally in 1989, which would lead to the creation of the Subaru World Rally Team (SWRT) in a partnership which continues to thrive today.

Under David's direction the team embarked on a programme, initially in the British, and subsequently the Asia-Pacific and World Rally Championships (WRC). In 1990, it was David who spotted the raw talent of up-and-coming young driver Colin McRae and later Richard Burns. He personally oversaw the development of their early careers, leading to two British titles for Subaru and McRae in 1991 and 1992, and a further title for Burns in 1993. Through the 1990s, Prodrive turned the Subaru into the icon of world rallying with its familiar blue and yellow livery. It was this success in rallying that is credited with helping to turn around the fortunes of the Japanese company. And the whole programme has been sponsored for more than a decade by BAT's 555 cigarette brand.

Richards also had contemporary F1 experience. In 1998 he was approached by the Benetton family to help turn around the fortunes of its team, which was at that point

⬇ **Thinking about the future. Jenson in the pit lane at Barcelona prior to pre-season testing with the BAR-Honda 005 in January 2003.**
📷 LAT

making heavy weather of its mid-grid status. It had been a long-time ambition of Richards to get into Formula One and he seized the opportunity. But after a year of mixed fortunes, David found that he was not given the opportunity to run the business in the way he wanted and returned to focus his attentions on expanding Prodrive at the end of the season. Benetton simply wanted a safe pair of hands to steer their operation. They weren't interested in the newcomer's views on strengthening the team's brand image or developing the driver line-up.

So it was hardly surprising that Richards thought twice when the mandarins at British American Tobacco approached him with the suggestion that he take over responsibility for the BAR-Honda squad. But, after some soul searching, he eventually agreed to take the job. But only on his terms.

"BAT, which was both part owner and sponsor of the team, approached me and asked me if I could come and help with this programme," said Richards. "So we went and talked about it at some length. I knew the people very well and could speak my mind. Can you take it over and run it for us? I told them I wasn't really minded to do this, but would write

> **Jenson chats with David Richards during the 2003 Australian Grand Prix weekend. The two men quickly established a good relationship.**
> 📷 LAT

thoughts down on one sheet of A4 paper and if we could agree something on those terms, then we could do it.

"I wanted the authority to get on with the job, really to do it the way I wanted to do it. I was very concerned by the fact that they had minority shareholders in there and a rather complicated situation. I didn't want to go in and rattle a few cages only to be thrown out after a short time. We needed the security, and finally agreed a five-year term.

"When we arrived we found a team which clearly had the right resources and all the finances, but had still grossly underachieved," he said. "In the main there was a lack of leadership and no clear vision of how to achieve their aims. There is a peculiar viewpoint in F1 that the more money and the more people you have will make your car go quicker. You have to know how to spend it to best effect."

Slipping into the BAR driving seat, Richards found that he had inherited Geoff Willis, the former Williams aerodynamicist, as the team's technical director – one of Pollock's more inspired recruits. Anxious to get costs under control, the new regime slashed the workforce from 450 to just under 400. It was certainly a start, but like a fully laden oil tanker attempting to change course, the delay between

pushing the rudder controls and feeling the ship respond can be agonising. Willis joined BAR early during the 2002 season, but effectively inherited the team's 004 design from Malcolm Oastler. Not until 2003 could he replace what he described as a "clunky, out-of-date, expensive to manufacture machine". At the launch of the BAR 005 in January 2003, he commented, "You have to start in a new ballpark and that's what we have done now."

Yet there was a hidden, nagging sub-text to Richards' position. How did he rationalise his relationship with Pollock and Villeneuve? Ideally, his end game was to dispense with the team's founder as, logically, he felt that having the old management team still hanging around the team's motorhome was not a satisfactory situation. Yet the structure of the BAR shareholdings was complex and intricate, so it would be 2003 before Pollock began to fade into the background and his presence in the paddock began to wane.

Yet Villeneuve started 2003 on a distinctly hostile note as far as Button was concerned. It was clear from his body language at the official launch of the BAR 005 that he didn't have much time for Button, believing his reputation to have been over-blown by the British media and emphasising that the Englishman still had to prove himself. He obliquely denigrated Jenson by references to his outgoing team-mate Olivier Panis who was switching to the fledgling Toyota squad.

"The key is whether you respect your team-mate or not," said Villeneuve. "If you do, as I did with Olivier, then everything is fine and nobody gets upset, but if you don't, then that can make things unhappy. He [Button] comes into the team seen as a future World Champion and I guess there's a lot of weight on his shoulders. I've won a World Championship in the past and people know what I can do. I believe it is important to be strong. You can't burst into tears if something goes wrong. That's one thing that I have a hard time to respect. Human strength is probably more important for respect than sheer speed."

In retrospect, it is difficult to see what point Villeneuve was trying to get across. Button certainly did not have a reputation as an F1 cry-baby and it looked as though the Canadian was the one who was feeling the pressure. For the first time in his BAR career he was squaring up to a team-mate who hadn't been recruited by Craig Pollock. Perhaps inwardly he knew that Richards was preparing to put his own personal form under intense scrutiny. The new team principal had inherited Villeneuve's water-tight $18 million contract for 2003 and it was clear that he regarded the Canadian – indeed any driver with such a price tag – as a luxury BAR could well do without.

Button, who was earning barely one-third of his team-

↑ **PR work can be tough! Jenson poses with a bevy of models for a sponsor's fashion shoot during the 2003 Australian GP weekend.**
📷 LAT

mate's fee, reacted coolly to Villeneuve's thinly veiled critique. He made it crystal clear that he wasn't about to be intimidated. "The press always likes to build up tension when a new driver joins a team, but I think we can work together," he said. "When you have the possibilities of winning you can fight each other, but we really have to work together to move this team forward and I am sure we can do that. I have had difficult team-mates in the past. Ralf Schumacher was tough to begin with, Jarno Trulli could be a bit hard, so that doesn't really bother me."

Pre-season testing was inconclusive. The new car was certainly a significant improvement over its predecessor, but Honda clearly needed to raise its game and had taken steps to do so. They ran an all-new V10 for the first time on the dyno in the summer of 2002. The engine initially looked very promising, but the development programme suffered a setback in the first race of the 2003 season in Melbourne after a problem with a batch of camshafts.

There was also an all-new Honda engine which first ran on the dyno in August 2002 and ran in a car right from the first Barcelona winter test. The policy was to upgrade it throughout the off-season, with a further five upgrades in power (giving between 0.3 and 2.0 per cent) and a reduction in weight totalling between 5 and 10 per cent over the year. In fact, they went back a step in Melbourne with the camshaft problem, but that was corrected by Malaysia.

Thus armed, Button and Villeneuve prepared to do battle in Melbourne, the first race of 2003 marked by the

↑ Jenson's debut
race for BAR at
Melbourne in 2003
was fraught with
tension after it
seemed as though
Villeneuve had
deliberately pitted
for fuel on the same
lap as he was
scheduled to
come in.

📷 sutton-images.com

introduction of a new one-by-one, Indy-style qualifying format. The running order of the Friday session was reversed for the crucial Saturday session, which would determine the grid positions. That second session on Saturday saw Jacques exerting the upper hand, the Canadian qualifying sixth on 1m 28.420s, just 0.2s ahead of Jenson.

"It's difficult to know where we stand compared with everybody else, but I'm pretty happy with eighth position," he reflected. "It's a good place to be starting the first race of the season. It wasn't a particularly great lap and like everybody else, there was room for improvement. We're starting from a points' scoring position, though, so I'm still feeling confident for the race."

The Ferrari F2002s of Michael Schumacher and Rubens Barrichello had buttoned up the front row of the grid, as expected, and surged away into immediate 1–2 formation, despite the initially patchy damp track conditions. But Jenson made a great start in the BAR and came round in sixth place, just ahead of Jacques, at the end of a satisfying opening lap.

The seamless Maranello machine may have looked on course for another dominant performance, but the reality of the situation was rather different. Barrichello was struggling with discomfort from his 'HANS' head and neck restraint system and spun off into the wall on lap six. The safety car was deployed to slow the pack while the debris was cleared and the track swept clean at the accident sight. On lap 12

the race proper restarted, but only four laps later Mark Webber's Jaguar lurched to a stop out on the circuit with a rear suspension problem. The car was judged to have come to rest at a potentially vulnerable spot, so the safety car was deployed for the second time.

The race was restarted again on lap 21 with Kimi Räikkönen's McLaren now leading Michael Schumacher, who was followed by David Coulthard's McLaren and the BAR-Hondas of Villeneuve and Button. At the end of lap 25 both BARs headed for the pit lane, a furious Button being subjected to a time-consuming delay as he queued up behind his team-mate.

"I had radio problems, so it was very difficult to communicate with the pit wall and both cars ended up pitting at the same time," said Villeneuve. "It took a long time to get the tyres working and I didn't get enough time on any set."

Button, who clearly suspected that Villeneuve had deliberately come into the pits in a bid to spoil his efforts, was certainly not amused. "Jacques did not come in when he was supposed to," he said. "I was a little bit shocked when he came in because I knew I was on the right lap. He did apologise, which was needed, I think. But I am not very impressed. It is very annoying. It was a bit of a nightmare for everyone."

Frustrating it may have been, but this was also an instructive psychological lesson for Button. In a peculiar way, Villeneuve had shown his hand. After adopting such a chippy, almost dismissively aggressive, attitude towards Jenson in the run-up to the season, one could almost discern that Jacques was now slightly on the back foot. If he was to have a future in a post-Pollock BAR squad, he would have to perform against this youthful incomer, almost ten years his junior. Suddenly that $18 million retainer looked less like an acknowledgement of Jacques's status as the 1997 World Champion, and more like an albatross of expectancy hanging heavily around his neck. Even at this early stage, Jenson seemed to be gaining the upper hand.

When he arrived in Kuala Lumpur ten days later to start preparations for the Malaysian Grand Prix, Button adopted a slightly amused and ironic tone as he reflected on the mishap in Melbourne.

"Yeah, the radios are fixed now, they work now," he grinned. "Mine's fine. After the race a lot of work has gone into making sure the radios are working well. Hopefully they will be good here. I feel I've settled into BAR very well and I feel very happy. The most comfortable I think I've been in Formula One and probably the team that I've been most happy with. Everyone seems very positive and

we're all working together very, very well. They have also listened to what I say from the word go, which has been very important."

On a slightly crisper note he later added, "To see a definite points finish, a very possible top-six place dashed because your team-mate decides to come in and refuel on the same lap that [you] had been told to, is, to put it lightly, frustrating. His explanation afterwards was that he had a problem with his radio at the precise time when I was coming in. He had no further problems afterwards."

Jenson also reflected on the fact that Sepang had been the scene of one of his best-ever races in the Renault 12 months earlier and he had high hopes for another strong performance in the new BAR. "I'm in it to win," he said firmly, "and finally I believe I am in a car that should consistently score points, might make a few podiums and could deliver my maiden victory. That's why I can't wait for this weekend in Kuala Lumpur. Just as long as my team-mate doesn't hold me up again!"

In the event the Malaysian race delivered rather less than was hoped for the two BAR-Honda drivers. Jenson at least had the satisfaction off qualifying ninth, three places ahead of Villeneuve, but the former World Champion didn't

⬇ **At a treacherously wet 2003 Brazilian Grand Prix, Jenson qualified 11th, but crashed heavily in the near-flooded track conditions on race day.**
📷 LAT

even make it to the start. Just before his car left the garage prior to the final parade lap, it developed an electrical problem. Then, at the start of the parade lap, the problem returned and damaged the gearbox. It seems that the main vehicle computer reset itself due a sudden voltage 'spike' through the system. That effectively scrambled the car's gear selection capability – the transmission attempted to select two gears at once and damaged the selectors.

There was a cruel helping of late race disappointment for Jenson as he dropped from fifth to seventh on the final lap behind Michael Schumacher's Ferrari and Jarno Trulli's Renault. "It was a very tiring race and the car was so difficult to drive," said Button. "I had very low grip and the oversteer got progressively worse towards the end. It destroyed the rear tyres. I held off Jarno for as long as I could, then on the last corner I braked where I normally would and the rear just locked up. I went straight on and Michael was able to get through."

Nevertheless, seventh place was a success of sorts. Included in the revised rule package for 2003 was a new points scoring system which rewarded the top eight finishers rather than the top six. So Jenson came away from Malaysia with two championship points, BAR's first of the new season. Villeneuve had yet to score.

Jacques rectified that situation a fortnight later when he dodged every hazard to finish sixth in the Brazilian Grand Prix at Sao Paolo's spectacular – and on this occasion, near flooded – Interlagos circuit. Even Michael Schumacher was caught out by the impossible conditions, but the fact that the world's greatest F1 driver of his generation made a slip was no consolation for Jenson who slammed off the road quite heavily.

The race was won by Jordan's Giancarlo Fisichella – one of Jenson's former team-mates – in circumstances so convoluted and bizarre that the Italian driver had to wait five days before the success was confirmed. It was ten days

before he eventually got his hands on the winner's trophy.

Fisichella was propelled into the limelight when Mark Webber, struggling for grip on worn Michelin rubber, crashed spectacularly coming through the fast left-hand kink before the pit. Webber's car ended up alongside the barrier on the left of the track, its driver shaken but unhurt, but debris was scattered all across the circuit.

As the dust settled, Fisichella ducked through the debris, but then Fernando Alonso – Button's successor in the Renault squad – arrived at speed over the crest and slammed straight into one of the Jaguar's wheels, which was lying in the middle of the circuit. That in turn slammed the young Spanish driver sharp right into the retaining wall. Both impacts were in excess of 30G and it said much for the standards of contemporary F1 car construction that Alonso escaped with nothing more serious than bruised legs. He was taken to hospital for a precautionary check-up.

The onset of heavy rain on race morning posed a serious potential problem for the Michelin runners, including McLaren, Williams and Jaguar. Their choice of designated race tyre was closer to a deep grooved full wet tyre than the relatively lightly grooved intermediate, which was available to the Bridgestone runners.

The FIA officials announced at 12.30pm, with almost painful formality, that a "change in climatic conditions had occurred." In other words it was now tipping it down, so teams were allowed to change various chassis settings and switch to rain tyres.

This edict notwithstanding, for a time it really looked as if the Brazilian GP might not take place at all. The cars were lined up on the starting grid, but the conditions seemed too risky to take the gamble. Eventually it was decided that the race would start 15 minutes late and that it would be run behind the safety car for the first few laps.

For nine laps the pack circulated steadily behind the safety car, then Bernd Maylander aimed the silver Mercedes CLK coupé for the sanctuary of the pit lane and the pack was unleashed with David Coulthard surging through to take the lead from Barrichello going into the first corner after the pits.

Going into lap 18, Ralph Firman's Jordan suffered a right front suspension breakage approaching the braking area for the left-hander after the pits at around 175mph. The errant wheel folded up onto the nose section of the yellow car and Firman became a passenger as it tobogganed into the back of Olivier Panis's Toyota TF103, eliminating both cars from the race. With debris all over the track, the safety car was deployed for the second time that afternoon.

Räikkönen stayed out behind the safety car, but the next ten cars all came in for top-ups while the pack was

"I FEEL I'VE SETTLED INTO BAR VERY WELL AND I FEEL VERY HAPPY. THE MOST COMFORTABLE I THINK I'VE BEEN IN FORMULA ONE AND PROBABLY THE TEAM THAT I'VE BEEN MOST HAPPY WITH"

JENSON BUTTON

still running at reduced speed. At the start of lap 23 the field was again unleashed with Räikkönen completing that lap 1.7s ahead of Coulthard with Michael Schumacher third ahead of Cristiano da Matta's Toyota, which had yet to stop, and Barrichello.

Even though the track surface was getting progressively drier by this point, rivulets of water were coursing across the circuit at turn three. On lap 25 Montoya became the first casualty of this slippery section, slamming off the road into the barrier. His Williams was soon followed by Antonio Pizzonia, then Michael Schumacher, on lap 27, also spun off the road, triggering the third safety car spell of the race.

On lap 30 the race restarted yet again, but only three laps later Button slammed off the road at turn three in what was a very heavy impact. "I just caught the standing water a little too much," said Jenson. "I tried to save it, but that just sent me into the tyre wall. I went in quite heavily and my back is aching a little, but it could have been much worse. It's disappointing, but that's the way it goes."

There was nothing more for Jenson to do than change out of his sodden overalls, nip back to the hotel for a quick shower and take a cab out to Sao Paolo's Guarulhos international airport for the long flight back to London. Two weeks ahead lay the San Marino Grand Prix at Imola and the start of the intensive European leg of the World Championship.

The BAR-Honda 005s performed well in qualifying at the evocatively named Autodromo Enzo e Dino Ferrari. Jacques lined up seventh, two places ahead of Jenson. "The first two sectors of my qualifying lap were okay," shrugged Button by way of explanation. "But then I went a little wide at the high-speed chicane up the hill and lost a bit of time. I also had a bit too much understeer on the high-speed corners."

This was a particularly emotional weekend for Jenson's former team-mate at Williams, Ralf Schumacher, and his brother Michael. They started preparations for the race knowing that their mother Elisabeth was critically ill at a hospital in Germany; the boys flew back in Michael's private jet to see her on Saturday evening. Sadly, she died that same night, ensuring that Michael's victory celebrations would be sober and muted when he scored his latest F1 victory the following afternoon. It was one of those personal tragedies that tend to put everything else into sharp perspective.

The Spanish Grand Prix at Barcelona's Circuit de Catalunya could also have been a good one. Jenson qualified fifth but there were five cars in front of him after his pit stop, so he felt he had to try to pass them. Audaciously, perhaps, he went down the inside of David Coulthard going into the 18th lap and he turned in. Button damaged the car and had to come in for a new nose. He finished ninth, two laps behind Michael Schumacher's winning Ferrari F2003. But Coulthard remained beached in the gravel and had to retire.

"In such circumstances it's perhaps inevitable that you both think you're in the right, so then you look at the video

↑ **Embarrassing moment! Jenson accidentally pushes his pal David Coulthard's McLaren off the road as he makes to overtake in the 2003 Spanish Grand Prix.**
📷 LAT

↑ **Marshals work carefully to extricate Jenson from his badly damaged BAR-Honda after his crash in practice at Monaco in 2003.**
📷 LAT

tape and say it's just a racing incident," said Jenson. "I mean we're good friends, so immediately after the race I went to his motorhome and we sat and watched it. We needed to sort it out, because we were flying back to Monaco immediately after the race – in his plane!"

The two British drivers duly shook hands and made up. Two weeks later, in what would turn out to be the last Austrian Grand Prix at the A1-Ring, Button finished fourth ahead of Coulthard. It equalled Jenson's career best result so far. "I had a great race today; I really enjoyed it," he said. "This is what the team really needed and deserved, but it wasn't a fluke. We really deserved our result today."

Finally, on the eve of the first practice session for the Monaco Grand Prix, Button revealed that his feud with

Jacques Villeneuve was finally over. The two men had been at loggerheads even before the start of the season after Villeneuve had insisted that Button had yet to prove his reputation on the track, then likened the 23-year-old Brit to a member of a boy band.

Button admitted that they had buried the hatchet and were collaborating to develop the new BAR-Honda 005. "I think we both said a few things that were a little bit pathetic," said Jenson. "But they had to be said. The thing is we are both very competitive. But we are working pretty well together now, which is good." David Richards added, "There was a little bit of friction between him and Jacques earlier on which we have managed to control now and point in the right direction."

"I'VE NEVER REALLY HAD A BIG ACCIDENT IN F1 BUT IT DOESN'T SCARE ME AT ALL"

JENSON BUTTON

much more of a thinking driver," he said. "Interestingly, while Jenson has certainly got the knack of this new one-lap qualifying format – pushing to the edge without making a mistake – Jacques is perhaps a little better at race set-up. But they are very well matched."

Yet hardly had this personal harmony been restored within the team than Button found himself out of the Monaco Grand Prix in an abrupt and fearful manner.

During the second practice session on Thursday morning, he lost control of his car coming out of the tunnel. It slammed sideways into a protective barrier at the end of the chicane escape road. The crash was a carbon-copy of Karl Wendlinger's terrifying crash in practice for the 1994 race, which resulted in the German driver being hospitalised and left in a coma for over a fortnight. Eventually Wendlinger made a recovery and raced again, but he never regained his F1 form and soon dropped from the senior formula to finish his career driving sports and touring cars.

Thankfully, the huge improvements in lateral cockpit protection – notably the high sided support structures now demanded as part of the F1 design process – meant that Button escaped with little more than concussion and a severe shaking. He also benefited from the latest seat technology available to F1 drivers, which means the seat can be removed from the cockpit in the event of an accident without having to remove the driver first.

A decade before the low cockpit sides of Wendlinger's Sauber made him painfully vulnerable in a high-impact lateral accident and he had to be lifted from the car and placed on a stretcher on the ground before the medical crew could work on him.

Button was taken to hospital where he remained overnight as a precaution. There was even talk that he might take part in the race, starting from the pit lane. In the event, wisely, he gave it a miss.

"I've never really had a big accident in F1 but it doesn't scare me at all," he said. "You never know if it will but it didn't scare me at all in this one. I'm looking forward to getting back in the car but I also don't want to be silly about it. I want to go through all the training regime first and make sure everything's good. I don't want to get back into the car and hurt myself. We have to make sure everything's okay before I do that."

That view was endorsed by Geoff Willis, the BAR technical director who worked with both drivers at Williams, albeit at separate times. "I am impressed at just how much both drivers have developed since I last worked with them," he said. "Jacques was always one tough cookie, but he is technically much better than he was at Williams. Certainly he is very sensitive – and better in the wet – and has clearly spent a lot of time thinking through his approach."

As far as Button is concerned, Willis said that he never had to be told twice about any technical aspect of the car during his debut F1 season in 2000. "Not only do I think he is faster than he was then, but now he's got such a library of experience to draw upon that he's turned into

→ Jenson and Jacques Villeneuve walk the paddock at Nürburgring, their earlier disagreements now apparently behind them.
📷 LAT

→ → Jenson could be a good sport. In the summer of 2003 he drove the author round Silverstone in this London cab for a feature previewing the British Grand Prix in F1 Racing magazine.
📷 LAT

→ Jenson comprehensively outclassed Jacques Villeneuve at Nürburgring for the European Grand Prix, qualifying 12th and finishing the race in 7th place.
📷 LAT

Button admitted he'd been pushing too hard. "What makes it so frustrating is that it was a bloody good lap," he told his father John when he visited his bedside later in the day. It certainly was a huge shame, as Jenson had been third fastest behind the two Ferraris during Thursday's first qualifying session and looked a strong contender on his fourth outing at Monaco.

"After I hit the wall I was unconscious. I don't know for how long. I sort of came round and they [the rescue team] had already cut [through the seat] up to my arm. I might have been awake but I can't really remember," he recalled. "I was speaking to [FIA medical head] Sid Watkins and he was saying that I was talking but I wasn't making any sense," said Button. "I said what's different? I mean, that's me all over. I didn't have a clue where I was. I was just looking down and my legs were hurting."

This unfortunate episode left Jenson ticking off the days until the Thursday morning before the Montréal race to hear whether he would be given the medical all-clear to compete in the Canadian Grand Prix. After the crash at Monaco, he had hoped to return to the cockpit for the following week's test at Monza. But he was examined by FIA medical delegate Prof. Sid Watkins earlier in the week and, on his advice, Button was persuaded to wait until Canada before trying to drive again.

"There was still some interruption to his memory when I saw him on the Tuesday after Monaco," said Watkins. "We are particularly mindful of the consequences of what we call the 'second impact' syndrome – where a driver suffers a second concussion a short time after the first impact." Under FIA regulations, the licence of any F1 driver who is hospitalised after an accident is automatically suspended until he his 're-integrated' after another medical inspection. In this case Button had to be examined by Watkins and the Montréal circuit's chief medical officer Jacques Bouchard.

Amazingly, Button's crashed car had already been totally repaired and Jenson was scheduled to race it in Montréal. "The structural integrity of the modern F1 car is quite remarkable, a testimony to the engineering of the teams and the safety rules promoted by the FIA," said BAR team principal David Richards.

In stark contrast, the structure of some personal relationships within the BAR team were beginning to look beyond repair. Eddie Irvine, the former Jaguar F1 driver, knew both Villeneuve and Button well and offered the view that the situation had become too complicated.

"I think this year Jenson's made a lot of mistakes and still has long way to go," Irvine said at Montréal. "But I have to say he's also made a lot of progress, is coming on well and has certainly been faster than I expected. On the face of it, Jenson has been blowing Jacques away, but you've got to ask yourself why. Well, Jenson has certainly grown mentally, but the fact remains that [Giancarlo] Fisichella had the extra pace to beat him at Renault last year. So has he suddenly got better, or has the environment Villeneuve finds himself in this year worked against him?

"To be honest, I think it's a bit of both. It's no secret that Jacques has problems with the team and it's certainly hurting him. He's upset with the way things have been handled and now he's got a situation where Jenson looks like a hero and he's got a team boss [David Richards] who doesn't want him in the car."

Richards' irritation over Villeneuve's $18 million contract for 2003 intensified as the season wore on. Put simply, he thought the money could be spent to better effect elsewhere. In a bid to redirect these crucial funds to the task of developing the car, he had earlier attempted to broker a deal which would have seen Villeneuve drive in the US-based CART series in 2003 before returning to BAR to see out the extra year of his deal in 2004. But this plan never reached fruition and Richards continued to make little secret of his frustration at having to pay so much for a driver who was not his first choice.

Richards did try to be conciliatory and positive towards Villeneuve in the run-up to the Canadian race, claiming that he had the ability to regain the form which carried him to the 1997 World Championship at the wheel of a Williams-Renault.

"For Jacques, it is psychological," said Richards. "It's been a tough start to the season for him with the number of retirements he's had. He knows he is still competitive and he knows that he has a competitive car. If it clicks at the right time, he will re-emerge as a real force to be reckoned with." But Villeneuve was above all else a realist. He acknowledged that he might have to accept a deal from a lesser team if an offer to renew was not forthcoming from BAR-Honda at the end of the season.

Whatever happened, Villeneuve faced a significant drop in salary from his current position as the second highest earner in F1 after Michael Schumacher. But he also had a reputation for being an independent free spirit who sought to limit his personal appearances and autograph signing sessions for the fans, something which could work against him in the future. He remained sanguine about that reality.

"The teams will do everything they can to bring down your value and your management will do everything they can to up it," he said. "That's just the market." The market in the middle of 2003 was certainly moving in Jenson Button's direction as far as consolidating the Englishman's status as an emerging star was concerned. He was asserting his edge over Villeneuve.

But the BAR-Honda package was generally neither quick enough nor sufficiently reliable through the summer of 2003. Neither car finished in Canada. Then Jenson comprehensively outclassed Jacques in the European Grand Prix before the Canadian retired with transmission trouble. But in the French Grand Prix he had to park his car out on the circuit, its tank run dry, after a problem with the team's refuelling rig meant that not enough fuel went in at a scheduled stop.

At Silverstone there was more disappointment. He qualified 20th, and last, after he clipped a kerb at Becketts and broke a front suspension push-rod. Under the circumstances, his climb back to eighth place was quite an impressive performance. That was followed by another eighth at Hockenheim, tenth in Hungary and retirement with a gearbox problem at Monza. But then came the US Grand Prix at Indianapolis and Jenson, although he failed to finish, was at least left with a broad grin on his face.

Button finished the season on a high note. He led at Indianapolis and again at Suzuka, where he finished fourth.

↓ Great day. Jenson forced the BAR-Honda into the lead of the 2003 US Grand Prix at Indianapolis, but its engine expired in the closing stages.
📷 LAT

← Jenson and new team-mate Takuma 'Darcy' Sato celebrate with the BAR-Honda team after finishing fourth and sixth at Suzuka in the 2003 Japanese Grand Prix.
📷 LAT

Earlier in the year he'd run strongly to finish fourth in Austria and repeated that in Japan, two places ahead of Takuma Sato, who replaced Villeneuve as his team-mate with one race of the season still to run. Yet it was the US GP that gave him the sense of anticipation that his long overdue place on the podium, his first top three finish, was at last within his reach.

"To be leading for 15 laps at Indianapolis was an amazing feeling," he smiled reflectively. "Okay, to be in that position we were really a bit lucky. We judged it correctly, switching to wet tyres when the rain was falling. Even though we weren't going to win, we still had a good chance of finishing second to Michael, although I think Kimi [Räikkönen] would have been quite close.

"In the wet we were pretty strong. I'd already gone through... you know, when you have tread on the rear wet tyres it's a big problem when the track is drying. I'd already gone through that process, but looking at Michael's tyres he still had to go through that. But I think I could have stayed pretty close to him in the wet. In the dry it would have been a different thing, but I think we would have been finishing second."

Ironically, despite the initial tension of their relationship, Jenson obviously felt quite reflective about Jacques when he realised at Suzuka that he was gone from the BAR-Honda equation, replaced by Sato. "It was strange once he had gone," he said. "Quite strange. And I found myself missing him really. It took me a little

time, but I eventually realised that he is quite a fun guy. Very opinionated, but quite funny at times. But I always suspected it might be a problem coming into the team at the start of the season, because there was quite a lot of press about me moving to the team and I knew that Jacques wouldn't like that."

So the 2003 season ended on a high note for Button, although the overall paucity of hard results inevitably looked as though it might lead him into that curious limbo land which bridges the gulf between a driver perceived as a bright young star and an established old hand. He developed a good relationship with BAR team principal David Richards who continued to insist that he was World Championship potential. The ease and assurance which Jenson radiated as he led those laps at Indianapolis served as a flickering reminder of what he might achieve given the right equipment.

Yet there was still that nagging question to be answered. Was Jenson Button really good enough to get the job done at the highest level?

"TO BE LEADING FOR 15 LAPS AT INDIANAPOLIS WAS AN AMAZING FEELING"
JENSON BUTTON

Mobil
LUCKY STRIKE
LUCKIES
555
WORLD RACING
LUCKY STRIKE B·A·R Honda
MICHELIN
HONDA
LUCKY STRIKE
J. BUTTON

[06]

RUNNING AT THE FRONT

Sir Jackie Stewart arrived in the paddock at Silverstone, three days prior to the 2004 British Grand Prix, in suitable style. Immaculately dressed, as always, he climbed from a black chauffeur-driven Jaguar limousine and briefly reflected that no fewer than 39 years had passed since he scored his own first Formula One victory, driving a BRM in the non-championship International Trophy race. In the process, he beat reigning World Champion John Surtees, in a Ferrari, into second place.

The question begging to be asked, even before Sir Jackie could don his carefully pressed tartan sports jacket, was could Button do the same in this year's British Grand Prix. Could he take the fight to another World Champion in a Ferrari, the great Michael Schumacher? Stewart weighed his words carefully, but his answer left no doubt that he was a huge fan of the young British driver.

"Jenson has all the qualities that make a Grand Prix winner and his time is sure to come," he replied. "Even if the challenge of getting on terms with Michael Schumacher's Ferrari may be too much for him to claim victory in front of what is expected to be a capacity 100,000-strong home crowd cheering him on at Silverstone tomorrow."

He also insisted that Button's status in the Formula One business had been enhanced by the fact that he overcame a serious streak of immaturity during his debut season with Williams in 2000 and that he was now one of the most rounded performers on the starting grid. "I think Jenson has surprised quite a few perceptive people in the business," he continued, "and by that I'm thinking of people like Bernie Ecclestone and perhaps even myself who felt that he progressed a little too far too soon.

"When Jenson got to the Formula 3 level, for whatever reason, I think he got a bit carried away with the rate of his progress. We met him and his people at that time when we were running [our own team] Paul Stewart Racing, but there were far too high expectations from all concerned at that time. There was no doubt that they saw in him something special, but the manner in which it was dealt with by his people, and even himself, suggested to me that it could possibly end in tears.

"His personal disciplines and manner of dealing with life showed a degree of immaturity, which I feared might not be removed as he developed. Having seen that at functions, and other activities, I feared he might not make the grade because of his mind not recognising the disciplines required to achieve in the big time.

"He has done a remarkable job in that respect, and that is probably the single most important element that has positioned him in what I think today has made him a potential winner of every Grand Prix this season. He drives well, he thinks well, he presents himself well, he behaves well and it's important for him that he retains those

← **A delighted Jenson celebrates on the podium after finishing second, behind Michael Schumacher, in the 2004 German Grand Prix at Hockenheim.**
Getty Images

qualities. I think he had started that process before David Richards [the BAR team principal] came along, but David has unquestionably added to it and confirmed in Jenson's mind what he needs to do to make the big time."

Yet Stewart also emphasised what a difficult psychological barrier it can be breaking through to win your first Formula One race. "The great thing you can say of every young driver is that he's got potential," he said. "But ultimately you have to translate that into winning..."

"It happened to me when I started in Formula One, but I had the benefit of knowing the disciplines I had to live with in order to be competitive in my shooting career before I ever started motor racing. Jenson didn't have that benefit, and it showed. But what he's done is collect himself very well and if he retains that focus, commitment and discipline, I think he has a tremendous future ahead of him."

Crucially, by the start of the 2004 season Button had developed a close working relationship with David Richards. It was not only professional, but also warm and suffused with mutual respect. Whether they would ever develop the sort of symbiotic partnership that Jackie Stewart enjoyed with the late Ken Tyrrell was another matter, but they had certainly grown very close and were capable of displaying the congenial informality that is usually only the preserve of genuinely good friends.

The author witnessed their lighter side during an informal dinner at the Richards's home near Warwick. We had been casually discussing the merits of the 2003 F1 rule changes for an interview that would form the basis of a feature in *F1 Racing* magazine when the BAR-Honda boss interjected firmly.

"God, don't ask a racing driver about whether or not the rules are good or bad," he said. "Ask a representative audience. The problem with this sport so often is that we ask the wrong people just how we should manage it. Instead, what we ought to be doing is the Oxford Street test!"

Jenson cocked his head slightly, looking politely confused; "What the hell was the Oxford Street test?" Richards replied firmly, "It involves picking 100 people at random walking down Oxford Street and asking their opinion. And I'll tell you another thing, if you put Jenson on one side of Oxford Street and Colin McRae on the other, I'll tell you who would be most frequently identified. He [McRae] may have won the World Championship, but it's a measure of F1's status that more people would recognise Jenson."

Ironically, as far as public recognition was concerned, Jenson's 170mph, brain-rattling accident during the first practice at Monaco in 2003 seemed to have boosted his profile more than any of his on-track achievements. "The worst thing is that people recognise me a lot more since Monaco," he said. "I found it all a bit unbelievable. When I got back to London, I went to see [Professor] Sid Watkins [the FIA medical delegate] on the Tuesday after the accident. That day I saw five people in HMV who came up to me and said 'You okay?' It was strange…"

Jenson admitted he had also learned to cope with his fans' intrusive nature. "It's quite scary when they come to your house," he said. "It doesn't happen very often, but it does now and again. And they even come to your motorhome. Somebody came to my motorhome at the Silverstone test when I was having a massage, knocked on the door and because I didn't answer, they just walked in. I said 'excuse me, what are you doing?' and she replied; 'I'm only here for one day', as if that was the answer. But generally everybody is very friendly."

But how much of a monkey on his back was the lack of a podium finish after four years competing in F1. "It's very tough, very annoying really," said Button. "Every time I have a chance, it's taken away from me through reliability problems. It's not that we've had a particularly unreliable year overall, it's just that when we've been in a crucial situation I haven't been able to finish."

Yet Richards made no bones about his belief that Jenson had what it takes to win a World Championship,

although he knows that raising BAR's game to the necessary level wasn't going to be easy. "I think in any relationship, if you have mutual respect, and have common goals, you can produce the result," he said. "I saw that with Colin [McRae] who seemed an unlikely World Champion at the time; everyone said it wouldn't happen. The same philosophy must work in the F1 business as well. But you've got to have clear goals.

"It's all very well looking up at the top of the podium and saying 'I'm going to be there,' but you've got to work out how you're going to get there and be realistic about how long it's going to take and the steps you're going to take to achieve it. I think that's part of the problem in motor racing. Everybody's looking for short-cuts and there aren't any . . . You can't just throw the dice and hope it will land the right way; it's a long, long process of determination and complete commitment.

"I just feel that Jenson is feeling 'Hmm, I've got to step up to the plate now. I'm the one who's going to lead this team'... That's going to put a lot of weight on his shoulders, but I believe he is up to it and that's going to change his approach as well."

← **Jenson relaxes in his motorhome during pre-season testing at Barcelona in January 2004.**
Getty Images

↓ **Keeping ahead of Fernando Alonso's Renault and the Williams of Juan-Pablo Montoya early in the 2004 Australian Grand Prix at Melbourne.**
LAT

First rostrum.
Montoya and
Michael
Schumacher give
Jenson the
champagne
treatment at the
2004 Malaysian
Grand Prix.
LAT

Cynicism, of course, is a journalist's stock in trade, and to say that predictions of the new BAR 006's potential were met with scepticism at the start of 2004 would be something of an understatement. But there was no denying their pre-season confidence. Much was made about the new chassis being stiffer with a lower centre of gravity. It had a smaller fuel tank to reflect the revised qualifying rules, a carbon-composite gearbox maincase and narrow, lightweight gear ratios, which would generate a substantial weight reduction at the rear of the car. But you still had to wonder. Without stating the obvious, everybody else offered wondrous predictions for their new cars' impending form. They couldn't all be right.

The author sustained his cynicism through to qualifying for the first race of 2004, the Australian Grand Prix in Melbourne. Jenson qualified fourth. When Richards told me that Button was not running with a light fuel load, I snorted, "I'll bet he makes his first refuelling stop before lap ten." In fact, he came in on lap 11. But it wasn't early compared with his immediate rivals. In the race, he came home a solid sixth. The team was also strengthened when Anthony Davidson was taken on as a full-time third driver. He regularly ran in the Friday free practice sessions, as permitted by the changed race weekend format for the new season.

"My start wasn't particularly great," Button said "and it was very slippery out there, but I managed to hold on to fourth for some time. Ralf Schumacher's Williams was able to get past me in the pit stop when we had a delay with the refuelling nozzle. Then [Juan Pablo] Montoya got past me out on the circuit. I think we need a little more in the way of race pace, but it's certainly a solid start to the season. We had good reliability, but then so did everybody else." The Ferrari F2004s of Michael Schumacher and Rubens Barrichello meanwhile finished in commanding 1–2 formation, setting the tone for a season which they would take by storm.

For Button, the key turning point would come at Malaysia's Sepang circuit where he would at last claim his first podium finish with a third place. He qualified sixth and was in the thick of the action from the very start of the chase, getting up to fifth by the end of the second lap after some wheel banging with Jarno Trulli's Renault R24.

Thereafter he never put a wheel wrong. The performance showed that both he and the team had significantly raised their game to challenge for World Championship points in

every race. "It was amazing," said Button. "The team has worked so hard. Obviously [it's] not the pinnacle of what we want, but a step in the right direction. I'm ecstatic."

Having qualified on pole position in conditions that saw the track temperature soar to 53°C, Schumacher capitalised on the slightly cooler conditions that prevailed on race day and pulled away strongly from the start. He had gambled to use the softer of the two Bridgestone tyre compounds, which gave him more grip from the outset.

Coming out of the final corner to take the chequered flag and wave to his pit crew, Schumacher eased off and Montoya closed to within 5 seconds. Yet most observers believed that the German driver's unflustered and composed style throughout the race concealed the fact that he'd held back from asserting his true potential advantage.

Button's third place was not without its problems. The only real moment came when he briefly had to ease off to activate the cockpit control which pumped more oil into the Honda engine from his car's auxiliary tank. His team-mate Takuma Sato had succumbed to an engine failure and the team was taking every precaution to ensure that a similar failure didn't jeopardise Jenson's race.

The most emotional moment of all came about ten minutes after Button emerged from the post-race media conference. As he jogged down the paddock towards the BAR-Honda team garage, he came face to face with his father John and the two men hurled themselves into each other's arms.

"HE DID IT ALL HIMSELF; HE DESERVES IT"

JOHN BUTTON

Since his boy's graduation into Formula One in 2000, Button senior had been a regular member of the Grand Prix scene. But he always stood quietly in the background, chatting with other regulars and never seeking to lay claim to any of his son's reflected glory.

"He did it all himself; he deserves it," said John Button, as Jenson was engulfed by the rest of the BAR squad. They jostled, cheered and reached out to touch the man who'd given them a taste of the respectability and credibility they had been craving since their debut in 1999.

Two years earlier he had been on course for third place at Sepang when his Renault suffered suspension problems in the closing stages and Michael Schumacher's Ferrari, climbing back through the field after an early collision, swept ahead of him on the final lap.

Now the moment had arrived, Jenson could hardly contain himself. "Melbourne was our first race on Michelins and we gained a lot of information to help us learn how to use them," he said. "Initially here we had too much understeer, and I didn't want to go into the race with an oversteery car. But we sorted that out, which was good.

"At the start, as we passed Mark Webber, I bumped

→ Celebrating
with the team
after finishing
third, behind the
Ferraris, in the
2004 Bahrain
Grand Prix.
📷 LAT

→ Golden
moment. Jenson
leads World
Champion Michael
Schumacher's
Ferrari at the 2004
San Marino Grand
Prix at Imola.
📷 LAT

wheels with Jarno [Trulli], which I worried might have damaged the car, but it was all fine. We've worked so hard and it's been a struggle to get on the podium for the first time. It's a fantastic feeling.

"I think the whole team has done a great job over the winter. We have really made a good step forward and that is [includes] everybody in the team. Everybody is really positive, which is great. There is not one person in the team that is negative and we are just making little steps forward every race, getting used to the tyres. We are really happy."

It was also a hugely satisfying result for David Richards. "Jenson and the team have worked very hard for this result," he said, "and to get his first podium finish in a straight fight with the best in Formula One is real proof of how far we have come."

The following night, still in Malaysia, Button went out for dinner with David Coulthard, the McLaren driver who was starting out on his final season with the team. "It was a special evening," said Jenson. "I get on with most of the drivers, but we don't hang out, and I certainly don't share the kind of conversations I have with DC. He said some pretty fantastic words about my race but, at the same time, it is very difficult for him. David has had an amazing career and he's been at McLaren nine years. And now it's not quite clear where he goes next. It's really tough. But he's still quick enough to win – if he gets the right car."

The third race of the 2004 World Championship was the inaugural Bahrain Grand Prix. It took place on the new

Sakhir circuit, another remarkable no-expense-spared constructional *tour de force* situated in the desert scrubland about 20 miles from the Sheikhdom's main city of Manama. Yet again Button's BAR-Honda proved to be the best of the rest as Ferrari's traditional rivals, Williams and McLaren, capitulated in the face of another Maranello grand slam.

When Button joined the two Ferrari drivers on the rostrum, they shared a heady non-alcoholic mix of rosewater and pomegranate juice rather than the usual champagne, in deference to the Arab protocol. The Englishman was third in the World Championship and confident there was more to come from both him and his team. "This is only our third race with Michelin tyres and working out how they work is not as easy as it seems," said Button. "We're gaining experience and hopefully by the next race we can make another step forward."

In Bahrain, Button had shared a villa at one of the luxury hotels with David Coulthard and his girlfriend Simone, and Mark Webber and his girlfriend Ann Neal. All three drivers get on really well and, despite his own disappointing race, David in particular had become a big fan of the 24-year-old. As they walked together towards the departure gate to catch their British Airways flight back to London on the evening after the race, Coulthard's generous grin as he escorted the similarly beaming Jenson was every bit as dazzling as that on the BAR driver's face.

And so to Imola, and the evocatively titled Autodromo Enzo e Dino Ferrari, the circuit in Maranello's heartland,

➜ **Getting closer!**
Michael
Schumacher
congratulates
Jenson on his
second place at
Imola, 2004.
📷 LAT

barely 50 miles from the Italian team's headquarters. Inevitably the 2004 San Marino Grand Prix was a moment for quiet reflection and private grief, marking as it did the tenth anniversary of Ayrton Senna's fatal accident while racing Michael Schumacher's Benetton for the lead.

The weekend saw a raft of tributes to the great man, who died when Jenson was just 14 years old. For many of Formula One's old hands, the events of that painful weekend were still etched in memory. But for guys like Jenson they were part of that tangled and complex tapestry that goes to make up the sport's history. Now it was time for the new guard to make its mark on the record book.

The pace in qualifying looked formidable and, for once, the Ferrari team looked under pressure. The sense of tension was palpable. Ferrari's charismatic president Luca di Montezemolo swung his agile frame on to the pit wall, dressed in open neck shirt and well-cut blue blazer, taking his place alongside the team's forever calm sporting director Jean Todt. This was the customary Maranello theatre, F1's equivalent of a royal visit. And Michael was expected to get the job done for the boss. With some justification.

A few yards further down the pit wall BAR-Honda boss David Richards hauled himself up onto the pit wall next to Geoff Willis. Their faces betrayed the faintest flicker of a smile – smiles of anticipation, perhaps.

The qualifying pace was startlingly quick. The early runners hovered around 1min 21s. Then Spanish star Fernando Alonso dipped down to 1min 20.895sec. Michael's expression tightened slightly. He'd set the pace with a 1min 20.440sec lap in the pre-qualifying session a little earlier, but Alonso was close enough to make him realise that Jenson might be even closer. Under the new qualifying format, Michael would run last having been quickest in pre-qualifying, so he would know the time he had to beat.

Montezemolo punched the air as Barrichello went quickest in the other Ferrari with a lap of 1min 20.451sec. Then it was Jenson's turn. With an economy of effort and meticulous deftness, the BAR-Honda slammed round in 1min 19.753sec. Michael Schumacher looked concerned. But finally he was on his way, tucked deep inside the cockpit of the scarlet Ferrari F2004. He was two-tenths of a second up going into the final sector of the lap. He pushed hard, but at the Variante Alta, a quick right/left chicane four corners from home, he just tried to carry a fraction too much speed into the turn. He slid wide, but gathered it all up in a moment. But it was enough to lose him pole position and he would have to be satisfied with second on 1min 20.011sec. Jenson had taken his first pole.

John Button was standing at the back of the BAR-Honda pit chatting to a group of Jenson's mates who were back in their local pub in Frome. Even over his mobile line, the

noise of their cheers and clanking glasses was deafening as Michael completed his slowing down lap, for once defeated in front of Ferrari's home crowd. Jenson was understandably ecstatic.

"It was a great lap and I enjoyed it very much," he said, with masterly understatement. "In pre-qualifying I was a little wide because I had very low grip, but in proper qualifying it seemed to be all there. We set the car up for the race, as everybody does, but we were lacking in qualifying a little bit. But qualifying, of course, is one thing, obviously winning a race is the main goal. I think that's going to be a little bit tougher than today's qualifying. But yeah, I'm looking forward to it. It's the first time in my Formula One career that I've had nobody in

front of me at the start, so it's all down to me now."

David Richards pulled out his now-trademark celebrational cigar and strode down to the back of the BAR transporter where all the mechanics were assembled. "Well done, guys," he grinned, shaking them all by the hands. "Six o'clock in the motorhome. A glass of champagne. But remember, we're not there yet. We're still aiming for the big one."

On Saturday there had been another bonus for Jenson as his girfriend Louise Griffiths arrived, fresh off a flight from Australia,with just enough time to give him a good luck kiss before he accelerated out onto the track to take on Schumacher.

After that long Sunday morning – somehow made

> ## "I THOUGHT HE WAS DRIVING IN THE DRY AND I WAS DRIVING IN THE WET. IT WAS THEN I REALISED THAT IT WAS GOING TO BE A VERY BUSY AFTERNOON"
> **MICHAEL SCHUMACHER**

interminable by the new format, which had eliminated a race day warm-up from the schedule – the moment finally came. Button's BAR took its place on pole position, fussed over with paternal concern by the army of BAR-Honda mechanics. As for Jenson, at last he looked slightly tense. His facial muscles were taut and he looked just a little pale as he pulled on his balaclava and fastened the chin strap on his helmet. One car length behind him Michael Schumacher looked ultra-calm and laid-back, chatting and smiling to friends and cameramen. There was nothing you could tell the six-times World Champion about high-pressure situations. He'd been through it all.

Button led the pack slowly round the final parade lap. He knew that his Michelin tyres would have more grip than Michael's Bridgestones for the first couple of laps, as the Japanese rubber took longer to come up to temperature. So when the starting lights flickered off, Button accelerated perfectly into an immediate lead as the pack jostled for position into the braking area for the Tamburello chicane.

While Button was making the perfect start from pole, Montoya accelerated his Williams-BMW up from fourth place to within inches of the World Champion's Ferrari as they jinked and weaved their way through the sequence of ess-bends on the outward leg of the circuit.

On the first straight Schumacher weaved across in front of Montoya to prevent him making an overtaking move, then pushed him off the road as he attempted to go around the outside of the Ferrari on the tricky uphill left-hand Tosa hairpin.

"Well, you know Michael had a poor start," said Montoya. "He was slow out of the first chicane, you know, the first turns two and three. I went to pass, he closed the door on me and I had to back off. Then he did the same out of the next corner and closed the door.

"So I went for the inside and I'm coming beside him and the next thing I see he's just coming straight at me, hit me and put me up the grass. It's very disappointing to see racing like that, but I'll be surprised if he gets away with it but it's up to the FIA." He added, "I actually got in front while we were braking and he says; 'Oh, he didn't see me there.' No chance. You've got to be either blind or stupid not to see me. But you know, it is racing."

Schumacher eventually escaped without penalty. Meanwhile, Jenson capitalised on the chaos behind him to open up a 2.7sec lead over the Italian car by the end of the opening lap. Perhaps inevitably, by lap four Schumacher had trimmed the advantage to 0.9sec, but Button refused to be ruffled by the pressure. Schumacher admitted he was impressed.

"It was mind blowing what he did in front of me," he said. "I thought he was driving in the dry and I was driving

in the wet. It was then I realised that it was going to be a very busy afternoon."

Button ducked in to make his first refuelling stop in 9.7sec at the end of lap nine; Schumacher piled on the pressure before making his first stop at the end of lap 11. When the race order settled down again the familiar order had been restored with Schumacher now 6.1sec ahead of the young Englishman.

Thereafter Schumacher held his lead without challenge through his second and third refuelling stop to beat Button by just over nine seconds after easing off on the final lap. Montoya finished a distant third, doubly frustrated by the fact that the new Williams-BMW was clearly unable to challenge the Ferrari F2004 in a straight fight, or the BAR-Honda, for that matter.

Schumacher's praise for Button's performance after the race was certainly satisfying, but equally warming were the positive words from Ferrari technical director Ross Brawn who had watched with fascination as the World Champion strained every sinew to hunt down Jenson in the early stages.

"It was an exciting start to the race because we didn't know quite how much fuel Jenson had on board," he said. "He stopped after nine laps, which meant he had 6kg less than Michael, and that was crucial. Michael blitzed his way around the extra two laps he was able to remain out before refuelling. That is why he got ahead and was able to control the pace. But it was, nevertheless, a very impressive performance by Jenson.

"BAR are serious contenders and they did a great job. Jenson had a good race. I am very impressed with him. The signs were there when he was at Williams and his present form just goes to show that when a driver gets the right engineers, the right environment and the team believe in him, then he raises his game. For him to have taken pole ahead of Schumacher was fantastic and he is learning to work with the team. He is going to become very hot property over the next couple of years."

Brawn then signalled Ferrari's possible future interest in the young English driver. "One day Michael is going to stop," he said, "and then we will have to look around for a replacement and see who is the best at that stage. Jenson will be on that list."

David Richards added his perspective to the praise flying around the Imola paddock for the 24-year-old. "This was another encouraging result for Jenson that doesn't surprise me because I have always believed in him," he said. "Michael Schumacher would have to make a mistake for Jenson to have a chance of beating him at the moment, but if he's second he has a chance to capitalise should that happen. I still believe he could win a race this year. We will be going to Spain in a fortnight and to other tracks throughout the season and expect to be competitive and do well."

Honda also saw this achievement as a major boost

for their own fortunes after a rough three years back in the Formula One firmament. In particular, Button's achievement in gaining pole position had something of a wistfully ironic symmetry about it. The last time a Honda engine had been on pole position was at the Canadian GP in 1992. On that occasion, it was Ayrton Senna in his McLaren MP4/7B who had set the pace. The engineer working on the Brazilian's V12 engine was none other than Takeo Kiuchi, who, in 2004, was Honda F1 project leader, or the chief engineer of the Japanese company's F1 programme.

"Jenson's achievement was immense," said the engineering director of Honda's F1 engine programme, Shuhei Nakamoto. "To take pole the way he did and then drive so strongly all race really demonstrates his ability and also his obvious confidence in the car. Although we have made a good step this weekend, we have to find the same again to challenge for the top."

Buoyed by this performance, the team moved on to Barcelona's Circuit de Catalunya for the Spanish Grand Prix. Disappointingly, Button's high hopes evaporated after he made a mistake on his qualifying run and could only line up 14th. Instead it was his team-mate Takuma Sato who kept the BAR-Honda flag flying with an impressive third on the grid behind Michael Schumacher's Ferrari and Juan Pablo Montoya's Williams-BMW.

Come the race, Sato finished a fine fifth, while Jenson climbed back through the field from his lowly grid position to set the second fastest race lap and finish eighth. "I didn't get a very good start and then I was a little disappointed with the first stint as it just wasn't possible to overtake," he said. "I struggled, to be honest. I lost so much time in the high-speed corners because when you're so close to the other cars you lose a lot of downforce."

The 2004 Monaco Grand Prix kicked off probably the most intense spell of F1 racing in the history of the World Championship. In the following eight weeks there would be no fewer than six races, culminating in Jenson's home event, the British Grand Prix at Silverstone. Ironically at Monaco, it was his former Renault team-mate Jarno Trulli against whom he was pitched in one of the most ferocious battles of his career; the outcome of the race remained in doubt almost to the final corner of the 77th lap.

At the chequered flag Button's BAR-Honda 006 was still 0.497sec adrift in second place after Trulli, who had started from pole position, stoically fought off every challenge the British driver could muster.

Both drivers rose to the challenge of this classic track. They started side-by-side on the front row of the grid and never made a slip throughout a race that claimed several of their more exalted colleagues. Most notably, Michael

Schumacher's Ferrari crashed into the barrier in the tunnel after a bizarre incident while running at reduced speed behind the safety car.

Button came to Monaco absolutely determined to make up for the slip at Barcelona. Truth be told, there was nothing to choose between Button's BAR and Trulli's Renault through the sunlit streets of the principality, but it was the Italian who just snatched pole after a scintillating lap on Saturday afternoon.

The safety car was deployed to enable Fernando Alonso's Renault to be dragged to a place of safety after rattling down the barriers to put him out of the race. Then Michael Schumacher's Ferrari, at the head of the slow-moving queue and still to make its second refuelling stop, became embroiled in a collision with Juan Pablo Montoya's Williams FW26, which broke the Ferrari's left-front suspension.

With the World Champion out of the race, it seemed as though Button would be successful in his efforts to hunt down the Renault driver as they headed for the chequered flag. From 5.5sec behind on lap 60, he trimmed Trulli's advantage to 4.1sec on lap 65, 3.5sec on lap 68, 1.6sec on lap 71 and, finally, 0.5sec on lap 74, with just three laps remaining. But he simply couldn't find a way to squeeze by.

"It was a tough and incredibly exciting race for me, and I suspect everybody watching at home too," said Jenson. "It felt great crossing the line in second place, but ever so slightly frustrating because I was only a second behind the winner. I didn't get a good start and [Fernando] Alonso was able to get by me. Then the traffic was very bad because of the back markers and I was getting really frustrated, being stuck behind [Cristiano] da Matta for three-and-a-half laps. After I broke free of them, I could really start catching Jarno. We had a great strategy today, but we just couldn't catch him."

At the Nürburgring a week later, Jenson finished a strong third in the European Grand Prix from fifth on the starting grid. This consolidated his third place in the Drivers' World Championship table with 38 points, two ahead of Trulli's Renault R24. "Considering the problem I've had with poor grip throughout the weekend, third place is a great result for me," said Button. "Obviously this podium [finish] was slightly more lucky than the other four, but a podium nonetheless. It was a tough race and I had problems with traffic again. I had to get past David [Coulthard] because he was holding me up by two seconds a lap, but fortunately he made a mistake at the last corner and I was able to pass him on the outside. A little bit brave, maybe, but it paid off."

Across the Atlantic for back-to-back fixtures at Montréal and Indianapolis, Jenson received an unexpected boost to

↑ Wheel to wheel.
JB gets close to his
pal David
Coulthard during
the 2004 European
Grand Prix at
Nürburgring.
📷 LAT

← Airborne over
the kerbs at
Magny-Cours
during the 2004
French Grand Prix.
Jenson finished
fifth after a
problem with the
BAR's anti-stall
mechanism
slowed him at his
final pit stop.
📷 LAT

his World Championship ambitions. He was promoted from fourth to third place in the Canadian Grand Prix after both Williams-BMWs and Toyotas were disqualified from the race after they were found to be fitted with illegal front brake cooling ducts.

Ralf Schumacher's subsequent exclusion moved Rubens Barrichello up to second place behind Michael Schumacher for a Ferrari 1–2 success. Button, meanwhile, moved up to third in his BAR. Juan Pablo Montoya's fourth-placed Williams and the Toyota TF04s of Cristiano da Matta and Olivier Panis, originally eighth and tenth, were also excluded by the FIA race stewards.

Even so, things hadn't looked particularly good during the race itself. "The race pace just wasn't there," said Button. "We came here looking for the win, but when it came to it we weren't quick enough, not even as fast as the Williams, which was a surprise."

The US Grand Prix at Indianapolis proved to be another disappointment. Button qualified fourth, one place behind his increasingly formidable team-mate Takuma Sato. In the race the team made a strategic error by not bringing them in to refuel when the safety car was deployed to slow the field after Ralf Schumacher's Williams-BMW spun into the wall at 170mph. Ultimately, however, such strategic nuances were irrelevant, as Jenson retired with a gearbox breakage after 26 laps.

Elsewhere in the BAR team, Anthony Davidson had been consistently impressive in his role as the team's third driver. The driver from Hemel Hempstead assiduously worked his way through the Friday free practice session gathering information on every technical parameter, ranging from tyre wear levels to engine performance and fuel consumption. Even allowing for the fact that the 'Friday testers' were allowed more tyres than the full-time racers, Davidson impressed everybody at Indianapolis by posting second fastest time behind Michael Schumacher.

"At the beginning of the year I was thinking, ah well, it looks like another year's testing for me because there's nothing else on offer," he said. "But I thought that perhaps this Friday job might play into my hands and it's turned out to be miles better than I could have ever hoped for. The car has been miles better than we'd ever dreamed of, what with Jenson getting pole position at Imola. We knew it was going to be good, but we're well chuffed.

"As far as my relationship with Jenson is concerned, it seems to go back as long as I can remember. I can't remember my life without Jenson Button's name being involved, probably since I was eight. We raced together pretty well non-stop in karting from the age of eight until 18, so being in the team together now is almost surreal, bizarre even.

"The strange thing is that, now we're in the same team, we talk about things which happened years ago when we were rivals, things we didn't talk about when we were in different kart teams. It's brilliant being here with him and I hope he feels it's brilliant having me here. We know each other so well we almost know what each other is thinking."

Returning to Europe, the French Grand Prix at Magny-Cours raised Jenson's hopes again, but after qualifying fourth he wound up fifth, disappointingly frustrated when the BAR's anti-stall mechanism accidentally engaged as he was accelerating out from his final refuelling stop. It slowed him by perhaps a second, maybe a second and a half, but races can be won or lost by such slender margins in today's ferociously competitive F1 environment. On this occasion it made the difference between him taking third, and a place on the rostrum alongside Michael Schumacher and Fernando Alonso, and his disappointing fifth behind Rubens Barrichello and Jarno Trulli, who nipped ahead of him as the BAR momentarily faltered.

Inevitably, the British Grand Prix at Silverstone generated a huge degree of hype and expectancy surrounding Jenson's prospects. As usual at European races, he stayed in his large motorhome tucked away discreetly at the back of the paddock, thereby eliminating the risk of any possible delays getting in and out of the circuit. In his mind it was just another race to be tackled with the same mental

discipline, concentration and focus as any other. But deep in his heart, he knew it was something special.

"Obviously, in terms of how I prepare for the race, I don't plan it any differently to the other 17 grands prix," he said, "so going to Silverstone will be the same as going to any other race. However, it is a singularly special experience to actually race in your home country. The British fans always

↑ **Jenson sported a new plain red and white helmet design for the 2004 British Grand Prix.**
📷 LAT

← **Running ahead of Rubens Barrichello's Ferrari in the 2004 British Grand Prix.**
📷 LAT

↑ **Shadowing Alonso's Renault during his climb back to second during the 2004 German Grand Prix at Hockenheim.**
📷 LAT

→ **Another second! Jenson celebrates with a balancing act at Hockenheim.**
📷 LAT

make the whole race weekend seem pretty incredible. In addition, ever since I first raced here as a boy, I have always loved Silverstone. It's very flowing and very quick, one of the original, proper undiluted F1 circuits, so I really enjoy it."

But it was that tangible emotional support from the fans that set the race apart in Jenson's mind. "To be honest, in Formula One the fans don't really make any difference to your performance or add any pressure," he said. "For footballers, runners or tennis players, they are close to the crowd and so much of their performance is mental. For them, the crowd screaming their support and getting right behind them can inspire them to raise their game, go that extra mile and push on that extra amount.

"In a Formula One car you can't really do that. You can't really push any more than you are already pushing because the crowd is cheering you on, and the car won't go any quicker because they are rooting for you. You obviously notice the crowds and the brilliant support and that's something I'm actually very grateful for, but it doesn't actually affect your speed on the day. You're pushing as hard as you can anyway.

"The parade lap on Sunday morning at Silverstone is when you really notice the fans cheering you on. It's great to see people supporting me and being patriotic with their Union Jack flags and team hats. Also, the noise is incredible. Even over the noise of my Honda V10, and with ear plugs in

and a helmet on, I can hear the air horns and the roar of the crowd. It's very special."

The characteristically capricious British summer weather threatened to turn qualifying at Silverstone on its ear. The format in 2004 meant that every driver did a single flying lap in 'pre-qualifying' and the reversed order of those times would dictate the running order in the battle for grid positions. In ideal conditions, a competitor needed to try ultra-hard in the first session to set quickest time. That would ensure he ran last in the crucial second session, getting out on the track when the grip was traditionally at its best and his prospects of a good grid position very strong.

But at Silverstone there were many teams whose weather forecasters predicted it would rain towards the end of the second session, so spectators were treated to the bizarre sight of some competitors running deliberately slowly in the first session to ensure they would run early in the second before the threatened rain arrived. Michael Schumacher even deliberately spun his Ferrari to waste time. Jenson, fastest in the first session, would go last in the second. Standing in the BAR garage he looked understandably concerned as the skies darkened.

However, David Richards stuck to his guns. "It won't rain," he said confidently. The team had a helicopter aloft monitoring conditions. And Richards was correct. Jenson had a dry run, qualifying strongly in third place behind Kimi Räikkönen's impressive new McLaren MP4/19B and Rubens Barrichello's Ferrari. Yet the race would prove to be a disappointment. The BAR 006 simply lacked the pace to challenge for victory and Jenson had to be content with fourth behind a Schumacher–Barrichello Ferrari 1–3, split by the gallant Räikkönen.

"We came into this race expecting a lot more than we've been able to deliver," shrugged Jenson. "Today's race performance was nowhere near our testing performance early in the year. We really struggled with a lack of grip compared to the Ferraris and it was like we were in a different race in terms of the way our car was handling. Our pace showed that we weren't as quick today as we were at the start of the season. Somehow we've managed to drop behind a bit, which is very disappointing, particularly in front of our own crowd. We have a lot of work to do."

That magical home victory had been denied Button just as it looked as though he would make the key breakthrough. Yet there was still a huge degree of confidence vested in him, both from inside and outside the BAR-Honda team.

"There is an understated quality about Jenson, almost as if he doesn't want to make a lot of noise when he's away from the car and that he would prefer that his performance behind the wheel spoke for his level of achievement alone," said Damon Hill, who tasted the glory of a home victory when he won the 1994 British Grand Prix at Silverstone.

"I think he could be the sort of driver who thrives on success. He obviously has the speed and the commitment to get the job done. He's in the position, at this stage of his career, when he wants to believe it will happen. But when you've been in Formula One you come to appreciate that there are no certainties.

"His big challenge now is to make it happen."

Two weeks after that rather disappointing run at Silverstone, Jenson found himself battling for second place in the German Grand Prix at Hockenheim, and he drove much of the race one-handed. Many people regarded it as the race of his life, better even than his performance at Imola three months before.

He eventually crossed the finishing line second behind Michael Schumacher's Ferrari F2004, still steadying his helmet with his left hand after the neck strap had worked loose and threatened to strangle him in the 180mph airflow 20 laps short of the finish.

Button grinned with exhaustion as he recounted the experience. "Towards the end of the race my helmet strap started to work loose and my helmet was lifting down the straights, which was pulling the strap tight against my throat and choking me. I had to drive one-handed for most of the time. I couldn't breathe very well and it was just more worrying than anything else. I was just slightly pulling it down to get more air in."

Meanwhile, in the pits the BAR engineers were busy examining Button's spare helmet on the assumption that their driver's problem was a loose visor. They worked out that they could possibly tape it down at the final refuelling stop, but when Jenson fully explained what the problem really was they simply kept their fingers crossed that all would be well. "This was without doubt the best race of my Formula One career," said Button, who had qualified superbly with the third fastest time. But after a ten-place penalty for an engine change during Friday practice had been invoked, he started the contest from a distinctly unpromising 13th in the final grid line up.

"I'm just so thrilled to finish second when I thought the best I could hope for was maybe fifth. The car felt fantastic, the engine was great and the teamwork from the boys was incredible.

"I made a good start but had a terrible first lap and didn't gain anything, but then the team did a fantastic job in the first pit stop. I had a great fight with Fernando [Alonso] who had incredible traction out of turn three where I was losing out to him, then on the straight I could get close to him again. I tried a few times to get past him and nothing seemed to work, but then I finally got him down the inside and held onto it."

[07]

HEADING FOR VICTORY

After his sensational race up through the field from 13th place on the grid to finish second in the 2004 German Grand Prix at Hockenheim, Button celebrated with the BAR squad, then vanished on a Mediterranean holiday. Then, just before 17.00 on Thursday, August 5, John Byfield, Button's manager, faxed a letter to David Richards informing the BAR boss that Jenson had signed for Williams in 2005.

Richards's PR offensive immediately went into top gear. Frank Williams, with characteristic discretion, wanted to keep the whole dispute under wraps. But Richards was having no truck with any such censorship. He was absolutely fuming that Button's management was apparently seeking to extricate the 24-year-old from his BAR deal by claiming that the option recently exercised to secure his services in 2005 and beyond was invalid.

"There is absolutely no question, we have a valid contract with Jenson," said Richards. "If anything I feel sorry for Jenson at the present moment for being so misled. Both myself and Geoff Willis, our technical director, have been attempting to call him for the last 24 hours, but without any success. This is a quite extraordinary situation."

Williams, who originally gave Button his F1 chance in 2000, remained confident that their new contract with the British driver was fully valid and he was contractually available to rejoin them next season. "There has been a long-term relationship between the Williams team and Jenson," said Frank Williams. "We have maintained that relationship until the present day, and I am delighted that one of the most talented drivers in Formula 1 has accepted the opportunity to return to the team."

For his part, Button added, "I am pleased that I had the option to rejoin the Williams-BMW team where my F1 career started. For the meantime the 2004 season has my full focus and attention. Beyond this, I have every confidence that the massive investment in resources and the depth of talent at Williams and BMW provides the best platform for my future ambitions to be a World Champion."

Williams added, "He has been under option to his present team BAR for some time. The option expired recently and Button's management called us to say that the option was no longer valid and would we be interested in his services – and of course I reacted as you might expect me to. I think they [BAR] probably wanted to take up the option but whether they've executed it or not will come out in due course."

Button's decision was underpinned by his belief that Williams, for all its short-term setbacks, was one of the established blue riband teams with the financial and technical firepower to blast its way back to a position where it could challenge for a World Championship. But Williams knew that BAR would not give up Button without a fight and would insist the whole issue be referred to the FIA Contract Recognition Board. The forum comprises a panel of three international lawyers who meet in Switzerland to

← At last! Jenson's expression says it all after his first Formula 1 win at the Hungarian Grand Prix in August 2006.
📷 LAT

adjudicate purely on the conflicting legal aspects of any specific contracts.

"It is our intention to enforce our current contractual position with Jenson," said Richards. "My duty is to the 400-strong workforce which has worked tirelessly over the past two seasons to give Jenson the car he has today; and to our partners, whose support and commitment to the team have contributed to the solid structure we now have in place. Unfortunately this is now a matter for the lawyers and I have every confidence that the legal process will confirm that yesterday's announcement has not only been premature but also invalid."

Williams said he believed that the BAR option was invalid and not exercised properly. "It all happened a few days before the German Grand Prix," he said. "Until then we had assumed that it was out of the question. It was a great surprise. It was an opportunity and we went for it. We have a contract with Jenson and we are of the opinion that BAR lost its opportunity to retain him. One fact is incontestable: Jenson wants and expects to drive for Williams-BMW in 2005 and 2006."

Williams declined to elaborate, but admitted that the Williams-BMW team had had "a form of option on Jenson since the end of 2000." He added that this had been lodged with the FIA Contract Recognition Board since the end of 2002 and said that this "was subsidiary to the BAR option."

For his part, Richards made it clear that Button would race in the Hungarian GP the following weekend as usual.

palmed off by claims from either Jenson or his management company, Essentially Sport, that BAR's option on the 24-year-old's services had somehow been incorrectly exercised.

Richards also made it clear that there was no question of standing down Button for any of the remaining races in 2004. "Jenson has a contract with us to the end of the year. The point of difference between us is whether or not he is committed for next year as well."

For his part, Button said, "Given the circumstances, the meeting was constructive. David is now in no doubt of my intention to return to Williams-BMW in 2005. My contractual position allows for this. I have also clarified that I am not moving for money, and my motivation is straightforward determination to win a World Championship. Essentially Sport were not permitted to hold private contractual discussions with BAR. I do not feel it was constructive for BAR to leak details of these discussions. Drivers are changing teams up and down the paddock at the moment – an accepted and fundamental element of our sport – and I wish that my return to Williams would have been less acrimonious in light of the contribution I have made to BAR this season."

An uneasy truce was eventually called between Button and BAR as team personnel began to assemble at the Hungaroring in preparation for the following Sunday's round of the Formula 1 World Championship. The race could conceivably offer Button his best chance yet of posting his maiden Grand Prix victory. The tight, twisty little track was expected to play to the strengths of the agile BAR 006 chassis and its impressively punchy Honda engine.

At the FIA press conference, Button was upbeat about his prospects for the race. "The atmosphere in the team is okay," he said. "It's fine. You know, we're all here to do a job and I am looking forward to it. As soon as we get onto the circuit we are in a position to challenge for a victory, I think."

"Some of the guys working on the cars may be disappointed with Jenson's decision," said one team insider, "but once the action starts out on track all that is pushed to one side. Their naturally competitive instincts kick in and they just want to be the best."

"The entire team left Germany three weeks ago on an immense high following what was without doubt the best race result in BAR's history," said Richards. "The race clearly underlined the fact that we had recovered our advantage over our immediate competitors and we can enjoy a very exciting fight in the remaining six races."

But the race itself proved to be a disappointment for Button. He qualified fifth and finished fourth. "I'm a little bit disappointed because we came here expecting better things," he said. "I think we might not have put the best

"We are all a team here at BAR, with one goal and one objective, which is to win races and World Championships," he said. "We must treat this matter as a little hiccup, nothing more."

Frank Williams refused to explain what went wrong with the BAR option on Button, but other sources said that it related to the timing of Honda's confirmation that it was committed to F1 on a long-term basis, one of the key assurances the Button camp was looking for.

Jenson finally met with Richards on Sunday, August 8, to talk over the events of the previous week. In a tense and uneasy exchange, Button explained that he was unshakeable in his determination to drive for Williams in 2005. But Richards made it clear he was not about to be

↑ **Michael Schumacher passes Jenson for the lead of the 2004 Italian Grand Prix at Monza. Jenson led for many laps before the two Ferraris passed him, relegating him to third.**

📷 LAT

condition of tyres on at the first stop, so we lost a lot of time. I had a lot of oversteer which made it very difficult to drive and that's why Jarno [Trulli] was able to get so close to me. Once I made the decision to put a set of conditioned [scrubbed] tyres on then the handling balance was much better."

With Takuma Sato following Button home in sixth place, BAR could at least console themselves that they had moved to within eight points of Renault in the battle for second place in the constructors' championship, a title clinched for the 14th time by Ferrari thanks to its latest dominant success.

Come the Belgian GP at Spa-Francorchamps, Button's efforts were for nothing as he eventually crashed out in spectacular style at 190mph going into Les Combes, his

right rear Michelin blowing out and pitching him straight into Zsolt Baumgartner's Minardi which he was lapping at the time. Thankfully neither was hurt.

By the time he arrived at Monza for the Italian GP, Williams had filed their 2005 contract with the Contract Recognition Board so the process of adjudication could now get seriously underway. In the race it finally looked as although Jenson's long-awaited maiden victory was on the cards. He led commandingly for many laps after both Ferrari drivers found themselves wrong-footed by the initially wet/dry track conditions.

In the end, however, Rubens Barrichello and Michael Schumacher stormed back into contention to finish 1–2 and relegate Jenson to third. "I just couldn't believe the way they drove past me on the straight without even trying," he said. "The pace of those two guys was untouchable. Their performance in the dry was staggering."

The Italian Grand Prix was followed on the calendar by the inaugural Chinese Grand Prix on the lavish new circuit at Shanghai, a race in which it seemed as though Jenson was right at the very top of his form with the BAR-Honda, and was poised to deliver a drive and result of genuine star quality.

Of course, dramatic scope for an unusual result was delivered in qualifying when Michael Schumacher spun off as he challenged for pole position, consigning the Ferrari team leader to the back of the grid. Tantalisingly, the door was now ajar for Jenson to score, be it whispered, his first

"I JUST COULDN'T BELIEVE THE WAY THEY DROVE PAST ME ON THE STRAIGHT WITHOUT EVEN TRYING. THE PACE OF THOSE TWO GUYS WAS UNTOUCHABLE"

JENSON BUTTON

Grand Prix victory – assuming, of course, he could kick the door hard enough to force it wide open.

Rubens Barrichello duly plucked the Maranello standard from Schumacher's faltering grasp to grab pole ahead of Kimi Räikkönen's McLaren MP4-19B, while the second row was shared by Jenson and Felipe Massa's Sauber. At the end of qualifying it was little exaggeration to say that JB seemed the happiest guy in the paddock.

Rubens knew it would be crucial for him to lead from the start, a task he just managed, but Jenson lost a place to Massa and completed the opening lap in fourth place. Jenson lost valuable time behind Massa and was 5.7sec behind leader Barrichello by the time he forced his way up to third place on lap three. Ahead of him now were the Ferrari, Räikkönen's McLaren and Fernando Alonso's Renault which had caught everybody slightly off-guard when the lights went out and vaulted straight through from sixth on the grid.

Button certainly impressed everybody with a confident overtaking move on Alonso on lap seven, and at the first round of refuelling stops it became clear that Jenson was opting for a two-stop strategy whereas most of his immediate rivals were running a three-stop plan.

In truth, Jenson's charge in the middle of the race was so impressive that, at one point, it seemed possible that his two-stop strategy might even genuinely endanger Barrichello's race lead. The Brazilian continued to punch in the quick lap times and, after Button's second stop, ran seven more critical laps on low fuel before coming in. Jenson had no answer, and when Rubens came out of that final stop 8.2sec ahead, the Briton knew that the game was up.

"When the gap started to get bigger by about one and a half seconds a lap, I thought we might be in trouble then," said Button. "When it got to 27sec on the pit board, I thought; 'I am going to push absolutely as hard as I can, but it's going to be very difficult to be in front when Rubens comes out of the pits.'"

In fact, over the final 14 laps, Barrichello backed off to such an extent that the Ferrari pit started to get a little nervous, but the Brazilian insisted that everything was under control and he took the chequered flag by just over a second from the hard-trying BAR-Honda driver.

"I always push very hard towards the end," said Jenson after another deeply impressive performance. "But I had to

⬇ **Second-placed Jenson leads Fernando Alonso's Renault at the Chinese Grand Prix at Shanghai in 2004.**
📷 sutton-images.com

→ **Jenson's Honda engine expires in a plume of oil smoke after just three laps of the 2004 season-closing Brazilian Grand Prix at Interlagos.**
📷 LAT

push 100 per cent to keep Kimi behind me [in third place]. It's also a circuit where you don't breathe for about 20sec every lap. You've got so many corners coming in such a quick sequence that you hold everything in. For the rest of the lap you are breathing pretty heavily."

He added: "It was a tough race, but it was great to get home on the podium. I thought we had a chance of the win, but when I was at the end of my second stint I was putting in some really good lap times, and it just did not come off."

Jenson was understandably anxious to sustain that form through the Japanese Grand Prix at Suzuka, even though he knew full-well that his BAR-Honda team-mate would be bursting with adrenalin to produce a strong performance on his home ground. Yet the 2004 Japanese Grand Prix would be remembered not for its on-track action, but for the fact that the circuit was closed, boarded up and firmly battened down – and all track activities on Saturday completely cancelled – due to the threat of a typhoon which seemed likely to blow through the area. Thankfully, it missed Suzuka and stayed, relatively harmlessly, out over the sea.

Qualifying, therefore, took place on race morning.

Michael Schumacher's Ferrari shared the front row of the grid with brother Ralf's Williams-BMW, with Mark Webber's Jaguar on the inside of row two ahead of Sato and Button. Jenson, running a heavier fuel load than his team-mate, stormed round the outside of Sato at the first corner, while Webber was also elbowed aside with the result that Button and Sato ran third and fourth, unable to keep pace with the brothers ahead, but edging away from the remainder of the pack.

Button pitted for the first time on lap 15, rejoining fourth just behind Sato, but since he'd now only got one stop to come rather than the two of his team-mate, he was clearly in very strong shape indeed. In the end he vaulted back into third place when Sato made his final refuelling stop, joining the Schumacher boys on the rostrum and further consolidating his third place in the world championship behind the Ferrari drivers, with only one race of the season to go.

In the run-up to the Brazilian Grand Prix at Interlagos, the last round of the title chase, Jenson heard that he would, after all, be staying with the BAR-Honda squad for 2005. The FIA Contracts Recognition Board had ruled that his contract with BAR for the new season was valid

→ **Jenson celebrates his third place in the 2004 Japanese Grand Prix on the podium with winner Michael Schumacher.**
📷 Getty Images

→→ **Jenson and David Richards at the end-of-season 2004 *Autosport* Awards in London, where Jenson received the International Racing Driver of the Year award.**
📷 Getty Images

and 'took precedence' over any contract with Williams. However, it was arranged that Jenson would move to Williams in 2006.

Just to bring Jenson down to earth with a bang, his Honda engine detonated in a cloud of smoke after just three laps of the Interlagos race. Still, he was a strong third in the Drivers' World Championship with 85 points, behind Ferrari duo Michael Schumacher (148 points) and Rubens Barrichello (114 points). Perhaps even more satisfyingly he was also ahead of fourth-placed Fernando Alonso who scored 59 points. A satisfying moment indeed!

For the 2005 season, BAR-Honda believed that it was well prepared. Buoyed by 11 podium finishes the previous year, buttressing the belief that they could really get close to winning a race with a little bit of good fortune, Geoff Willis and the rest of the technical team worked hard to produce a much more sophisticated car in the form of the BAR 007.

The new machine featured a second-generation version of the team's neat carbon-fibre gearbox, there was a significant weight reduction and, now with Honda as a 45 per cent stakeholder in the team, the promise of top-notch V10 power units to cope with the new rules requiring that engines lasted for two races between changes. There were also new aerodynamic regulations to be accommodated, and this seemed to be where the car came unstuck.

"We thought initially we were well prepared for the

2005 season," said Willis. "As it turned out, I don't think we did a terribly good job of responding to the change in aero regulations. This really compromised a lot of our pre-season testing, in which we knew that we had what looked to be an aerodynamic characteristic problem. We struggled for quite a while to fix it." Yet there were to be even more serious setbacks to bug Button and the team's progress throughout what was really a bitterly disappointing campaign.

Jenson started the season with an eighth-place grid position for the Australian GP at Melbourne, this being the first time that Saturday and Sunday morning's times would be aggregated to establish the grid order. It was not a development that met with universal approval. As Jenson's mate David Coulthard, now driving for the Red Bull-Cosworth team, remarked; "I don't think this is what this sport stands for." Button, meanwhile, had to be content with a distant 11th place in the race, on a day when DC took a very respectable fourth place on his first outing for his new team. That was not really the way Jenson had seen it working out.

Then it was off to Malaysia for the second round of the title chase. Jenson arrived in Kuala Lumpur after an intensive physical training programme in Brunei. For this race the second BAR was taken over by test driver Anthony Davidson, as Takuma Sato was sidelined by an unpleasant stomach bug. Jenson suffered an engine oil leak during Saturday free practice, which meant that he had to use set-up data from Davidson – whose settings he found too oversteery for his taste – and he could line up no better than ninth.

Jenson was hard pressed even to talk about the race. The failure of oil pressure sensors on the Honda engines resulted in Button and Davidson shuddering to a halt after a couple of laps. Jenson was back in the pits, changed out of his overalls, by the time eventual winner Fernando Alonso's Renault came in for its first refuelling stop. Surely things could only get better. Couldn't they?

They could, and they did at the next round in Bahrain. In the sweltering heat Jenson qualified a poor 11th. But he was up to fourth by the time he came in for his second refuelling stop, only to encounter a major problem with his BAR's gearchange mechanism. After a painfully long stop, Button was duly push-started back into the race, scattering one of the team's jacks as he aimed back towards the race track. But he barely made it to the end of the pits.

"I got a reasonable start, our car felt strong and we had good pace, so we were hoping for better things" he said. "I tried to overtake Fisichella on lap two, but he moved across me and I lost three places behind him. From about

20 laps we were beginning to experience some bad gear shifts and also some signs of brake wear, so I had to look after the brakes a bit more."

He added; "The pit crew removed the tyre to inspect the front left at the last pit stop, and it seemed it would make it to the end of the race. When I tried to select first gear and pull away, the clutch problem recurred. The guys did a fantastic job to try and get me back in the race, but the car just stopped at the end of the pit lane."

Then came Imola and the San Marino Grand Prix, the first round of the title chase to take place in Europe. Jenson qualified third behind Alonso's Renault and Räikkönen's McLaren, and ran strongly through to take an eventual third at the chequered flag. Things were looking up for BAR-

Honda, and their revised aerodynamic package certainly seemed to be paying dividends. But there was a painful sting in the tail of the weekend's events.

Only hours after the end of the race, the FIA took the extraordinary decision to appeal against the stance of its own stewards who had given Button's BAR-Honda 007 a clean bill of health at the post-race scrutineering session after the race.

Button's car spent a protracted six-hour spell in the scrutineering bay being examined in detail by FIA officials. The car was weighed immediately after the race and tipped the scales at 606kg, comfortably above the 600kg minimum weight limit, but after it had been drained of fuel it weighed only 594kg. Despite this, the scrutineers

accepted the explanation from the team and duly confirmed the provisional race results.

Some observers whispered that the BAR 007 may have been fitted with a concealed 'secret' fuel tank which could retain fuel pumped into the car at the final refuelling stop of the race, the better to keep it above the minimum weight limit when checked. However, the team responded by claiming that this was nothing more than a collector tank for the Honda engine's high-pressure fuel pump.

The FIA court of appeal hearing – against its own officials' decision, remember – was scheduled for the Wednesday before the Spanish Grand Prix at Barcelona. When the verdict was announced, it resonated through the paddock at the Circuit de Catalunya like a thunder-clap.

↑ Jenson at the wheel of the BAR-Honda 007 during its official launch at Barcelona in January 2005.
📷 LAT

The BAR-Honda team was handed a three-race suspension, including disqualifying Jenson from the San Marino GP, plus a suspended six-race ban which could be triggered if, over the balance of the 2005 season, the team was found guilty of any other rule infringement.

Initially BAR team principal Nick Fry said he was "appalled" by the decision of the four-man court in Paris, and made it clear that the team would seriously consider legal action in the civil courts to seek redress. Historically, of course, this has been shown in F1 circles to be a road to nowhere, as the civil courts are very reluctant to overrule decisions made by sporting governing bodies.

Max Mosley, the FIA President, commented: "The facts of the case are very clear. The team was asked to pump the fuel out of its car. It left 15-litres in the tank and told us it was empty. Under the circumstances, we feel BAR has been treated rather leniently."

The court stopped short of endorsing the FIA's contention that BAR had committed a fraudulent act in concealing the details of an apparently hidden fuel tank on Button's car, but concluded the team had displayed "a highly regrettable negligence and lack of transparency." Button would now not be racing at either Barcelona or at Monaco. It was a ruling which hurt. Badly.

Button and the BAR squad made their return to the championship at the Nürburgring for the European Grand Prix. The team was in an upbeat frame of mind, determined not to dwell on their passing frustrations. They had been running fresh Honda engines at Imola five weeks earlier, so these had been sealed by the FIA and stored at Honda's Bracknell base before reappearing installed in the BAR 007s at the Nürburgring.

Button and team-mate Sato had to make their qualifying runs on a dusty track, allied to the fact that their undertrays were carrying an additional 6kg of ballast to make doubly sure there would be no repeat of the scrutineering problems. Jenson was unable to better 13th on the grid.

Come the race and Jenson was nowhere, never in the hunt, and finally finished 10th. "We thought we would be reasonably strong here, so today's race has taken us by surprise," he mused thoughtfully. "We had a lot of oversteer in the car, but also, on turn-in we had massive amounts of understeer, so don't really understand what was going on. I struggled a lot, but at least we made enough progress to move a bit farther up the grid in Montréal."

It was certainly a prophetic observation. During their unwelcome interregnum, Honda had been testing extensively, successfully back-tracking to a chassis set-up they had evolved at Mugello earlier in the season. It did the trick and Jenson outqualified Schumacher's Ferrari to take fastest time by 0.2sec.

"I'm thrilled to be back on pole," said our hero. "The past few months have been difficult for all of us at BAR-Honda, and everyone has worked so hard to turn our performance around. It felt like a good lap, but the circuit had quite low grip, so I was a little surprised, to be honest. I don't know if we are quick enough yet for the victory, but it will be interesting to see how far we can take today's result."

The answer came quite quickly – 'not quite far enough.' Jenson moved legitimately at the start to block Schumacher's Ferrari, but both men were swamped on either side by the fast-starting Renaults of Fisichella and Alonso. The BAR team leader therefore completed the opening lap in third place, ahead of the McLarens of Juan Pablo Montoya and Kimi Räikkönen, while Schumacher had to be content with fifth.

Button's BAR was running light, making its first refuelling stop on lap 15, ten laps before Fisichella and

"I'M THRILLED TO BE BACK ON POLE. THE PAST FEW MONTHS HAVE BEEN DIFFICULT FOR ALL OF US AT BAR-HONDA, AND EVERYONE HAS WORKED SO HARD TO TURN OUR PERFORMANCE AROUND"

JENSON BUTTON

Montoya came in from what were now first and second places. The upbeat mood lasted until lap 47 when, battling with Schumacher for third, Jenson ran wide exiting the fast chicane before the pits, slamming into the right-hand retaining wall.

From the BBC *Radio Five Live* commentary box overlooking the final corner, BAR test driver Anthony Davidson heard the flat burble of Button's traction control cutting in unexpectedly as his car skipped over the inside kerb, throwing him out too wide to make the corner.

Davidson had the words out of his mouth in warning almost before the car slammed off the track, leaving Jenson's World Championship points tally still firmly stuck on zero. He was furious with himself.

"It was completely my mistake," he said. "And it was very frustrating because we were looking good. My start wasn't great and the Renaults got better traction off the line, which allowed them to leapfrog me. But we have to take

→ **A lighter moment as Jenson celebrates taking pole position for the 2005 Canadian Grand Prix at Montréal.**
📷 Getty Images

↓ **Jenson crashed out of the race at Montréal after running wide while battling with Michael Schumacher for third place.**
📷 Getty Images

the positives out of the weekend and try to build on those for next weekend at Indianapolis."

Not that Jenson got the chance to display much in the way of sporting prowess at all when it came to the US race. Behind the scenes there had been civil war in the paddock. In the aftermath of a high-speed accident involving Ralf Schumacher's Toyota, caused by a Michelin tyre failure going through the slightly banked Turn 13 during practice, the tyre supplier eventually conceded that the tyres available for the race could only be guaranteed if the speeds were reduced on the approach to Turn 13.

It was quite simple; without such a change to the circuit they could not risk racing. The FIA felt unable to offer – or pursue – a compromise way out, and the net result was that only six Bridgestone-shod cars – from Ferrari, Jordan and Minardi – took the start, much to the vocal displeasure of the disgusted US crowd who traditionally expect rather better entertainment. Jenson had qualified third behind Jarno Trulli's fuel-light, pole-winning Toyota and Kimi Räikkönen's McLaren. That was all rendered academic, of course.

The next race on the calendar was the French GP at Magny-Cours, which thankfully left Jenson celebrating his

first helping of championship points that year. He qualified seventh, and finished fourth after a solid performance. "It's also a real boost as we prepare for our home Grand Prix at Silverstone next week," he enthused. "I think we had a very good strategy here and the team worked hard all weekend to achieve fourth place today."

Sure enough, qualifying through Silverstone's high-speed swerves played to the strengths of the BAR 007 chassis. He wound up second on the grid behind Fernando Alonso's Renault, much to the delight of the partisan home crowd.

"We got everything we could out of the car in qualifying," said Jenson. "The car struggled a bit through Copse and Becketts, which has been a bit of a worry, but it is working very well in the low-speed corners." In the race he faded slightly to finish fifth. He was ahead of both of the Ferraris, admittedly, but it had been Montoya's day in the McLaren-Mercedes as far as victory was concerned, with Fernando Alonso coming home second for Renault. Not bad, but a long way from what Jenson had been hoping.

Signs were that the BAR 007 was definitely improving. At Hockenheim, Jenson squeezed on to the front row of the grid alongside Kimi Räikkönen's McLaren-Mercedes, after Juan Pablo Montoya spun on his qualifying run, wiping out the likely prospect of a McLaren 1–2 in the eventual starting line-up.

The race went well enough. Räikkönen dominated from pole, but the McLaren proved disappointingly fragile and

succumbed to an hydraulic failure while comfortably in the lead. In handing the race victory to Alonso and Renault, Räikkönen's retirement also wiped out any lingering prospect of the Finn winning the World Championship.

Montoya made up for his qualifying slip by climbing back up to second at the chequered flag, followed across the line by Jenson, who had done well to get the upper hand in a wheel-to-wheel battle with Michael Schumacher's tyre-troubled Ferrari.

Then came the Hungarian GP and more problems for Button. It seemed almost unbelievable for those of us on the touchlines, but barely 12 months after propelling himself into the glare of the spotlight while trying to leave BAR-Honda for Williams-BMW, here he was suddenly now trying to get out of his Williams contract for 2006 in order to stay where he was.

There was logic behind this seeming madness. Jenson wanted to stay with a team that had a works engine contract. He'd signed his Williams deal in the belief that they would be continuing in partnership with BMW, but by the middle of 2005 it was clear the wheels were falling off that particular alliance. Williams would be using customer Cosworth engines in 2006 and Button, believing these would be insufficiently competitive, wanted out.

"I suppose it is ironic," mused Jenson with masterly understatement. "But I need to be in the best position I can be, with the best team. I've been in F1 for six years and I haven't won a race. I want to win races and fight for the

↑ Jenson leads Michael Schumacher's Ferrari on his way to third place in the 2005 British Grand Prix at Silverstone.
📷 sutton-images.com

Jenson drove to an excellent third place in tricky conditions at the 2005 Belgian Grand Prix.
📷 LAT

Jenson prepares for the 2005 Japanese Grand Prix at Suzuka on the grid, while his PA, Jules Kulpinski, keeps him cool.
📷 LAT

With Dannii Minogue at the *Elle* Style Awards in January 2006.
📷 Getty Images

World Championship and I cannot afford three years to build up another team.

"To be strong in F1 you need a works engine manufacturer. I found out that Honda was so committed, and was going to buy 45 per cent of the [BAR] team only after I had made my decision last year to go for Williams. It was definitely a mistake to sign a contract so early, and I was a little misguided, but that's ultimately my responsibility."

Jenson then took a deep breath and acknowledged that it would obviously make life a little 'sticky' for his friendship with Sir Frank Williams, but he felt he was making a firm point by risking it in order to demonstrate just how much he wanted to stay with BAR.

Yet Williams brushed all these apparent reservations aside. Not only was he slightly baffled by Button's vacillating, he was also not in the mood to let the young man off the hook without one hell of a fight.

"No amount of money will make us change our mind," said Williams. "Jenson could have been better advised. Williams has a fully binding contract. There is no let-out clause. It is very clear and straightforward. There needs to be a clear understanding of the word 'commitment'. Once you give your word, you should keep your word."

He added: "I recognise that where he presently is, the team is doing well to very well. But then I look at the coming season [2006] and the order will almost certainly shuffle. Williams is a strong team with a strong past, a weak present and, certainly in my own mind, a strong future. It is as well resourced as any team and I do not overestimate. And Jenson is part of that." Williams closed his comments by saying that Williams was looking forward to seeing him in its team again "because it has a right – and a proper and correct legal right – to expect him to be here. English law is as clear as it comes."

Words can sometimes – make that often – come easily in the F1 business. Six weeks after Williams and Button adopted these trenchant positions, what everybody was confidently expecting to happen all along duly came to pass. Button agreed to pay somewhere in the region of $30m to Williams over five years, reputedly, to get off the hook.

"Trust me, it hurts," said Jenson in reference to this huge financial commitment. But there was now a firm spring in his step as he faced the future, confident that Honda would be able to give him the tools necessary to get the job done. By an admittedly convoluted route – which nobody could have foreseen – they did just that!

The intervening weeks had seen Jenson repeatedly and consistently gathering World Championship points. Fifth from eighth on the grid in Hungary, then fifth from 13th at the inaugural Turkish Grand Prix at Istanbul, eighth at Monza and then a brilliant third from eighth on the grid at a

> ## "THERE NEEDS TO BE A CLEAR UNDERSTANDING OF THE WORD 'COMMITMENT'. ONCE YOU GIVE YOUR WORD, YOU SHOULD KEEP YOUR WORD"
>
> **FRANK WILLIAMS**

rain-slicked Spa-Francorchamps. Jenson drove with great maturity and dignity in these fraught conditions, although he was given a leg-up to the final place on the podium thanks to Montoya's McLaren colliding with Antonio Pizzonia's Williams-BMW on the final lap of the race.

At Interlagos, fresh from negotiating the release deal with Williams, Jenson capitalised on a revised aerodynamic package to qualify fourth behind Alonso's Renault, Montoya's McLaren and the remaining Renault of Giancarlo Fisichella. The race turned into a dominant Montoya–Räikkönen McLaren 1–2, with Alonso coming home third to clinch his first World Championship title.

Jenson trailed home seventh, the ecstasy of doing the Williams deal quickly evaporating after a poor performance overall. "It was a difficult day for us," he admitted. "Our pace was slow and we suffered a tyre graining problem from the start of the race. We were on the hard tyre as well,

so we didn't expect that, in fact that's why we took that tyre. I struggled with oversteer for most of the way." Tenth-fastest race lap told its own story, and Button could have certainly been forgiven a 'what-might-have-been' moment as he watched Alonso and the Renault squad celebrating their championship success.

There were only two races left now, neither set to deliver Jenson much in the way of consolation. At Suzuka, for the Japanese Grand Prix, he qualified second to Ralf Schumacher's Toyota on a patchy damp track, and briefly managed to poke his BAR-Honda through into the lead during the second round of refuelling stops. He wound up fifth, beaten to fourth by Mark Webber's Williams-BMW. The BAR again lost its handling edge as the race progressed, and his cause was not helped when the car's fuel flap refused to open when he stopped on lap 22, losing him six seconds as the mechanics had to open it manually.

Finally, the season was rounded off with eighth place in the Chinese Grand Prix at Shanghai. By then Jenson had climbed to ninth place in the Drivers' World Championship, albeit a massive 96 points behind newly crowned champion Alonso. There was nothing for it but to settle down and start all over again in 2006.

Into the new year, Jenson Button seemed to have found a fresh equilibrium. He had a new manager in the form of the amiable and calm Richard Goddard, and a fresh yardstick by which to judge his own performance in the form of his new team-mate Rubens Barrichello, fresh in from Ferrari where he had fulfilled the role of impressive team-mate to Michael Schumacher.

Here was meat and drink for the F1 pit lane theorists. If Button could thrash Barrichello, then bearing in mind that Rubens occasionally gave Michael a genuine scare, then perhaps Jenson was as good as the seven times champion.

Taken as a whole, 2006 would offer a shaky start for Button and BAR-Honda, but deliver a happy ending. Half-a-dozen races into the season most people were seriously starting to wonder if Honda had been out of their minds paying a reputedly modest $30m to buy the 55 per cent balance of the BAR shareholding. Either way, the car was now branded a Honda RA106.

However, although the initial testing form demonstrated by the new car was undeniably promising, mid-way through the season the whole project had become so badly unravelled that technical director Geoff Willis was soon consigned to a factory-based role. He left the team mid-season, by mutual agreement.

There were new rules to be considered as well at the start of 2006. Instead of having to make one set of tyres last through qualifying and the race, it was now possible to change tyres once again, but subject to using a maximum

of seven sets for each car over a Grand Prix weekend. The old breed of 3-litre V10 engines was replaced by a new generation of 2.4-litre V8s, and there was a new 'knock out' qualifying format, culminating in a top ten 'shoot out' for the first five rows of the grid.

The opening race of the year this time took place in Bahrain, where Button qualified third behind the Ferraris of Schumacher and Felipe Massa. The nature of his race on the sand-swept torrid Sakhir circuit was dictated by a clutch problem which caused him to make a poor start. "Had I not had such a bad start, this could have been a great race for us," he reflected after finishing an obviously disappointed fourth. "The pace of the car was absolutely there, but the strategy did not pan out because we were not where we needed to be when it came to our pit stops." Alonso won from Schumacher and Räikkönen's Ferrari.

By this stage in his career Jenson was looking confidently for his first win, so while places on the podium were all very well, he was now of a status where he was expecting more – very much more. After Bahrain, moving

"I'M OBVIOUSLY PLEASED TO BE BACK ON THE PODIUM. BUT IT WAS THE TOP STEP THAT I HAD IN MIND"
JENSON BUTTON

on to Malaysia the following weekend raised the prospect of his first GP victory. But the Renaults of Alonso and Fisichella were just too strong – third was the best he could manage.

"I'm obviously pleased to be back on the podium," he shrugged, "but it was the top step that I had in mind, so we [the team] are a little disappointed. We want to be winning races, and today showed that we are in the fight, but there is still a lot of work to be done before we can achieve that target."

At Melbourne, for the Australian GP, Jenson shone brightly to take a dazzling pole, despite struggling for grip early in a qualifying session punctuated by a rain shower and gusting wind. "It's fantastic to take pole position after that," said Jenson. "We juggled with the differential and the traction control settings, plus the tyre pressures and the front wing adjustments, and then the car was very good on new tyres right at the end."

The race was chaotic. Away from the start Alonso almost ran into the pole-sitting Honda as they accelerated away from the grid, but he quickly had to tuck in behind

↑ **Jenson started from pole position for the 2006 Australian Grand Prix, but faded in the race. His Honda engine failed in spectacular fashion as he approached the finish line on the last lap.**
📷 LAT

the Englishman, as the safety car was immediately deployed after Massa crashed his Ferrari at the first turn. Alonso jumped Button on the restart, but the safety car was out again from laps seven to nine after Christian Klien slammed off the track in his Red Bull.

At the second restart it was Räikkönen's McLaren which vaulted ahead of Button. It was the start of a long steady drift back through the field to fifth place, then a sudden drop to 10th as his Honda V8 expired in flames coming out onto the startline straight to take the chequered flag.

"The tyres were not too bad when they built up temperature," he shrugged disappointedly, "but in the long periods running behind the safety car they lost all grip. Coming through the right-hander onto the pit straight

it was as if we had no wings on the car. There was nothing I could do about it."

Come the San Marino GP at Imola, Button ran second with the Honda from the start, dropping only 3.7sec to Schumacher's leading Ferrari by the time he brought the RA106 in for its first fuel stop at the end of lap 15. He dropped to seventh, but he was back to third by the time he came in for his second scheduled stop in the Italian sunshine on lap 30.

It seemed as though everything was going to plan when, due to a misunderstanding, the chief mechanic Alastair Gibson, holding the 'lollipop' indicating that the driver should remain stationary with his foot hard on the brake pedal, raised the sign and Jenson assumed it was time to rejoin the battle.

As Button began to accelerate, Gibson suddenly noticed

that the fuel hose was still connected, so he brought the lollipop down with a bang on Jenson's passing helmet. Jenson immediately slammed on the brakes, but already the nozzle had been torn off the end of the fuel line, so it was a miracle that the whole thing did not ignite. In the chaos several team members were knocked off their feet and, after a mechanic had successfully removed the refuelling nozzle from the side of the car, by the time Jenson was back in the race he had dropped to seventh with no prospect of recovering a podium finish.

Another Honda engine failure sidelined Button in the European GP at the Nürburgring, then it was back to a distant sixth-place finish at Barcelona, his Honda not still quite *au point*. "The car worked well, and it was pretty much a faultless race," he said in summary. "But I was behind Rubens in the first stint and Räikkönen was able to pull away. But in clear air the car was as good as it has been probably since Malaysia. I was reeling in Kimi for fifth in the closing stages, but there was not quite enough time left."

Monaco was a total nightmare. He qualified 13th, trailing home 11th beset by terminal oversteer. Oil leaking over the rear tyres spun him out of his home race at Silverstone after only eight laps, then the nightmare continued with ninth in Canada and a retirement with accident damage at Indianapolis. Then it was an engine failure in France, followed by a close fourth at Hockenheim – certainly better. But it was all muscle flexing. Jenson was only part of the supporting cast. It seemed as though nothing could break this endless cycle of not-so-near misses. Until the great day arrived.

Finally, after seven years of frustration, near misses and mounting pressure to prove his pedigree, Jenson Button stormed to the first win of his F1 career in the 2006 Hungarian Grand Prix at the Hungaroring, the tortuous little track just outside Budapest.

Traditionally this race is held in sweltering, airless

summer heat, but on this occasion it was transformed into a lottery by heavy rain just before the start, allowing the Somerset-born racer to showcase the benefits of his smooth driving style by bringing his Honda home half a minute clear of a depleted field.

Yet the final 18 laps seemed impossibly tense for the 26-year-old strapped snugly into the cockpit of the mud-streaked car number 12. From the moment that the World Championship leader Fernando Alonso steered his Renault off the drying track with a transmission breakage at the start of lap 52, this was a race Button could only throw away.

Ahead of him stretched the narrow, twisting ribbon of Hungaroring tarmac that normally renders overtaking all but impossible. Almost 13sec behind was the Ferrari of Michael Schumacher, struggling in vain to defend his own position as his tyres deteriorated.

So Button kept looking forward, his senses razor-sharp, monitoring every noise and vibration for any hint of trouble.

↑ **Ahead of Fernando Alonso again during the 2006 San Marino Grand Prix at Imola. Jenson finished seventh after a chaotic pit stop during which he left the pit with the fuel hose still connected.**
📷 LAT

← **Another 2006 retirement, this time at Silverstone after an oil leak over the rear tyres caused Jenson to spin out.**
📷 LAT

→ Diving inside Michael Schumacher to take fourth place early in the 2006 Hungarian Grand Prix. Jenson would go on to score his, and the Honda team's, debut Formula 1 victory.
📷 LAT

⬇ Jenson takes the chequered flag to win in Hungary.
📷 LAT

Coolness personified, he did not want the race to end. The far more nervous faces belonged in the pits, where Button's Honda crew also craved a first victory for the seven-year-old team, to rectify what to this point had been a dismal season.

With the end of lap 70, the long, long wait was over. With the entire Honda pit crew lining the pit wall cheering and waving madly, Button accelerated cleanly out of the final uphill 180-degree right-hander, exploding out onto the pit straight to take the chequered flag.

"Wow, what a day, it's amazing," said a wide-eyed Jenson as he stepped down from the podium. "The weather conditions made it very difficult, but the team has certainly deserved it. I just did not want the race to finish."

So ended the longest period without a British driver winning an F1 Grand Prix, some 65 races and more than three years having passed since David Coulthard won his final race for McLaren at Melbourne in 2003.

"With about ten laps to go, after we had turned the engine revs down, I let it sink in," Button said, underlining his remarkable coolness in the cockpit. "Personally, being selfish, the first thing you think about is yourself. But the team have really worked for this.

"This takes a big weight off my shoulders and I must offer a massive 'thank-you' for all my fans' support during the bad times. It's really nice to be able to repay them with this success. Our car worked very well in the wet, but I don't think we necessarily won by being the fastest car. We had the right strategy."

That said, Button had started the race in deep frustration. After that encouraging fourth place at Hockenheim, his renewed optimism went up in a cloud of V8 smoke and flame during Saturday's free practice. His Honda engine blew up so spectacularly that the session had to be red-flagged in order to clear up the debris. It cost him a ten-place grid penalty for having to change his engine, with the result that he started the Hungarian race from the outside of the seventh row.

Yet by the end of the opening lap he was splashing round in 11th place, the Honda felt good and by lap five he had moved up to seventh. On lap seven he was fourth behind Alonso's Renault, the Spaniard having climbed through the field from 15th on the grid to sixth on the

opening lap. But neither Alonso, Schumacher nor Kimi Räikkönen – who crashed his McLaren into the back of Vitantonio Liuzzi's Red Bull – would reach the end, and Button profited.

"On the first lap I had a terrible start," he said as he sipped the victory champagne. "But then I settled down to pick off people, moving closer and closer to the front. To come from 14th place and win could hardly be a better way of scoring my first Grand Prix victory.

"The only problems were judging the conditions, knowing when to switch to dry tyres, something which other people made mistakes with. It would be nice to party tonight, but I'm going off to Shanghai for some PR work tonight, so the holiday and partying will have to wait."

↑ **The eyes have it. An ecstatic Jenson is a Grand Prix winner at last.**
📷 LAT

[08]

CHARACTER BUILDING

It took some time for the Hungaroring success really to sink in. It had been a bruising couple of seasons for Jenson when one took into account both the legal spat with his team over the supposed Williams deal, followed by the technical controversy which had caused the disqualification of both Jenson and BAR from those three races during the course of 2005. But now the monkey finally seemed to be off his back and the unfolding ribbon of tarmac beneath his wheels surely beckoned him on towards more Grand Prix success.

Yet those in the F1 pit lane were quick to appreciate that there was more to this success than met the eye. Jenson had always radiated a pleasantly gregarious personality, laid-back and assured without being in any way superficial. He had always been a straightforward kind of a guy, but now his character assumed a freshly polished sheen of confidence. If you watched him stroll down the pit lane there was a fresh spring to his step, post-Budapest, no question about it.

At a stroke he now had the opportunity to bury that early-season catalogue of disappointing performances. The ignominious engine failure at Melbourne, the red faces after he pirouetted on his own oil at Silverstone. They could now be consigned to the sepia-tinted past. Or so they hoped. Now he would barnstorm through to the end of the 2006 season with a fifth, three fourths and finally a terrific third place at Interlagos, where he came roaring through from

14th on the grid to finish third after grappling with traction-control problems during the qualifying session.

Fourth place in the Turkish Grand Prix at Istanbul Park followed on from that glorious afternoon in Budapest. It was good enough. In a straight fight, the Honda RA106 was no threat to the Ferraris or Renault which finished ahead of Jenson, but he easily saw off Pedro de la Rosa's fifth-place McLaren-Mercedes, which was in itself pretty satisfying. But it was clear that Button's car would need something of a helping hand from circumstances if it was to nudge its way up to the sharp end of the finishing order again.

Fifth place at Monza was similarly distant, although he crossed the finishing line 10sec ahead of Honda team-mate Rubens Barrichello. Then it was fourth from fourth on the grid in a rain-soaked Chinese Grand Prix at Shanghai, some lucky breaks in traffic with backmarkers – or shrewd manoeuvring, if you prefer it! – helped Jenson make up some unexpected ground on a day when Barrichello unfortunately locked up his brakes and slid into Nick Heidfeld's BMW, losing both of them a lot of time.

Yet another fourth place at Suzuka rounded off the Japanese GP on a successful note, particularly from seventh place on the starting grid. "We had a solid race and I think we did the best job possible given the fight going on for the championship," said Jenson. "We just haven't got quite enough to beat the two contenders [Ferrari and Renault] right now, but we will get there, trust me!"

← Jenson contemplates the season ahead before the 2007 Australian Grand Prix at Melbourne.
📷 LAT

↑ **Battling with Giancarlo Fisichella on the way to fourth place in the 2006 Japanese Grand Prix.**
📷 LAT

↓ **BAR's swansong in Brazil, 2006.**
📷 LAT

In a sense, you could say that Jenson kept the best until last. At Interlagos, where Michael Schumacher was rounding off his illustrious F1 career at the wheel of a Ferrari, Jenson's climb through the pack was highlighted by a great overtaking move on Kimi Räikkönen's McLaren on the way to his final podium position of the 2006 season, on a day when Felipe Massa had become a home-town winner and Fernando Alonso World Champion for the second time.

"A massive well done to both Felipe and Fernando," said Jenson generously. "After yesterday's problems it's a great

result to come from 14th to third, a great way to end the year, and one of the most enjoyable races I've had, fighting through the field."

When the dust finally settled on the bumpy, rutted and rather threadbare Sao Paulo circuit, Jenson had ended the 2006 Drivers' World Championship in fifth place on 56 points, less than half title-winner Alonso's eventual tally. Honda was fourth in the constructors' championship table on 86 points, beaten by Renault, Ferrari and McLaren. It was promising, but in real terms not really quite good enough.

Nevertheless, by the end of 2006 Jenson was obviously a young man now comfortable in his own skin. His considerable wealth had secured him a flat in Monaco, and his father John, by now one of the great F1 paddock favourites, was also enjoying his retirement nearby.

"Old Boy," as Jenson affectionately calls his father, was described with brilliant precision in the *Sunday Times* as "having the dark leathery tan and the voice of an East End gangster." Jenson noted: "He's a bit of a legend down here. I'm working non-stop and he's playing all the time." John always stayed in the background, content to watch his boy from a respectful distance. As things turned out, he was going to need as much support from his father, his team and his wide circle of friends, as he could get.

Honda was confident it could maintain its late-season '06 momentum through the following year. Yet although the initial wind-tunnel results looked promising, they did not correlate to the RA107's performance once it rolled out onto the circuit.

"It was quite clear from the start that the RA107 had a pretty serious aerodynamic imbalance, with the centre of pressure effectively moving backwards and forwards under acceleration and braking," said team principal Nick Fry. "We really identified the problem at the early-season Bahrain test, and it was our view that it was a problem which could be overcome. But the figures were fairly horrific and the whole problem was more complicated than we originally thought."

The season opened with Lewis Hamilton understandably taking the lion's share of the media attention in the Australian Grand Prix at Melbourne. Kimi Räikkönen won the race for Ferrari, while Fernando Alonso and Hamilton were second and third for McLaren-Mercedes, Lewis driving absolutely faultlessly in his first F1 outing.

Button finished a lapped 15th. His frustration with the Honda RA107 reached fever pitch during what was a fruitless 57-lap marathon. Over the radio link to his pit crew he shouted that the car's handling was rubbish and so bad that it was almost impossible to drive. In return, the Honda technicians came up with the not-very-helpful view that their data suggested that Jenson was mistaken.

It was not a reaction calculated to enhance the mood of the moment.

Jenson was becoming obviously and extremely frustrated with the Honda team. Even Bernie Ecclestone noticed. The F1 supremo offered the view in Malaysia that 2007 might well be a crucial season for the British driver, and he needed to put his annoyance to one side and power through the difficulties.

"Jenson really must get his act together this year or he's going to find the future very difficult," said the billionaire. "He needs to stick with Honda, get his head down and make it work. Okay, so his current problems may not be his fault, and it's a shame they've happened, but he's just got to get things back on track."

That was easier said than done. Once again, it was Lewis Hamilton who hit the high notes for McLaren in Malaysia, coming home runner-up to his team-mate Fernando Alonso. Jenson was left to emerge from the cockpit in a dejected frame of mind again after struggling home 12th, this time behind his team-mate Rubens Barrichello.

Then it was on to Bahrain for the third round of the title chase. In the desert heat things were set to get very much worse. He was out on the first lap!

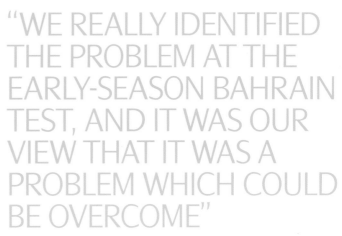

"WE REALLY IDENTIFIED THE PROBLEM AT THE EARLY-SEASON BAHRAIN TEST, AND IT WAS OUR VIEW THAT IT WAS A PROBLEM WHICH COULD BE OVERCOME"

NICK FRY

Jenson could hardly believe what was happening to him. "I made a good start and made up at least three places," he reflected. "But then Taku [Sato] ran wide, tried to squeeze me and I had nowhere to go but onto the dirt on the inside. Then on turn three I had Coulthard and someone else fighting around me. DC went wide, then cut in sharply and I had nowhere to go (again). We touched, I spun around and the anti-stall didn't cut it. I stalled and that was the end of my race after two corners."

Back to Europe and there was no better luck awaiting Jenson and his Honda. At Barcelona's Circuit de Catalunya, home of winter F1 testing, he was 1.6sec slower than Felipe

← Through good times and bad, 'Old Boy' John Button has always been his son's Number 1 fan and supporter.
📷 LAT

Massa's pace-setting Ferrari. It was the difference between pole position and an eventual 14th on the starting grid.

Come the race, the experience degenerated into another fiasco. Jenson knocked his wing off against Barrichello's rear wheel, had to pit for a replacement and lost a lot of time. Then came Monaco, the scene of his splendid second place to Trulli three years earlier, but again the RA107 just wasn't up to the job.

Button lost out in the familiar opening lap mêlée at Ste. Devote and, running with a heavier fuel load, could only chase Barrichello home 11th. "It was a difficult race today," he said. "I was stuck in traffic in all three stints and never got a clear run, so I couldn't make the best advantage of our strategy. But we have to take some encouragement from our signs of improvement. We have to keep pushing and moving in the right direction."

Hope and optimism are as much an F1 driver's stock-in-trade as pure driving talent. It's the same for the senior design talent and engineers. Understandably, during the bad times, there is a tendency to seize on small morsels of positive news and interpret them in the mind's eye as having more significance and worth than perhaps they deserve.

Yet it was a forlorn hope. Grinding away relentlessly to find tenths of a second a lap was going to make it a gruelling and painfully drawn-out season.

In Canada, Jenson's Honda suffered gearbox problems on the grid and didn't move away from the startline. He was back in his civvies long before Lewis Hamilton took the chequered flag to notch up his maiden Grand Prix victory. A week later Jenson was 12th, a lap down, as Hamilton won again at Indianapolis, surviving a spectacular involvement in a first-lap collision.

Then it was back to Europe again where eighth place was Jenson's reward for a strong drive in the French GP at Magny-Cours. "It was an enjoyable race today, and we've shown that the car has improved a lot," said Button. "It's nice to have a car that gives me the confidence to push, and I'm pleased with our fastest lap relative to our competitors. A good weekend, and I'm looking forward to another one at the British Grand Prix next week."

Fair enough. At Silverstone Rubens and Jenson translated 14th and 18th on the grid to ninth and 10th at the chequered flag. They were the only cars running on a one-stop strategy, which meant the drivers had to struggle with a heavy fuel load in the opening stages of the race. "They were the most improved drivers in the race, having made up five and eight places respectively," said a team statement.

As previously suggested, there's nothing like looking on the bright side. But that didn't help at the Nürburgring, venue for the European Grand Prix, where Jenson skidded out of the race on a rain-soaked circuit after just three laps.

Arriving in the paddock at the Hungaroring just 12 months after he dodged every kerb and mastered every puddle to take his maiden F1 victory, it was as if it had never happened. Unwittingly, Jenson found himself starring in a fleeting cameo which threw into sharp perspective just how relentless and uncompromising professional sport can be.

Friday's free practice session for the 2007 race had just taken place, and a flood-tide of photographers and television reporters swept across the 'boulevard' separating the back of the pits from the grandly titled McLaren 'brand centre'. At the centre of this group was Lewis Hamilton, McLaren's new star and the media darling of the moment.

In the crush, nobody noticed Jenson as he ducked and weaved a path through the seething mass of humanity. Last year's winner, seemingly yesterday's news, he walked alone and almost unrecognised by the jostling onlookers.

"To be honest, I don't really feel anything about being here again," he said. "In a sense it's nice to be hoping for the conditions to be the same as they were last year, but the real test will be to see whether this year's car might be a bit more competitive on a tight and twisty circuit, just as it was at Monaco earlier in the year."

For the moment, Button had to make the best of the opportunities presented by the current Honda to showcase his own talents, sending out fortnightly reminders that he was 27 years old, with eight years of F1 experience under his belt.

"The Hungaroring is a track with a good rhythm and a good mix of slow-speed and high-speed turns," he said. "It was never really one of my favourite races before, but for obvious reasons that all changed last year. It will always be a special place as the scene of my first win. Obviously it will be quite a different race for us here this year, but hopefully we can keep up the steady progress we have been making and take another step forward,"

He added: "A lap of the Hungaroring is quite tiring because there is no respite and no opportunity to relax your hands, so you are gripping the steering wheel hard the whole time. Although last year's race proved rather a wet exception, the Hungarian Grand Prix is typically a hot one, and the relatively low speed means the airflow over the driver is reduced, so you never really get the chance to cool down. It's quite a physical challenge, to be honest."

During the course of the race weekend, the author plucked up the courage to ask him what was increasingly looking like the obvious question: "Isn't the truth of the

⬇ **What a difference a year makes. Twelve months after his debut victory, a dejected Jenson watches from the side of the track at the 2007 Hungarian Grand Prix after another retirement.**
📷 LAT

matter that it's about time you considered ditching Honda and trying to find a drive somewhere else?"

He responded with a well-judged blend of humour and irony. "That's easier said than done," he said. "Where, precisely, would I find another drive?"

Later in the season, several seasoned commentators noticed a subtle change in Button's personality. After a bitterly disappointing season, he began to radiate a slightly detached, curiously enigmatic approach to his dilemma. It was almost as if he wanted to skim over the surface when reflecting on the 2007 campaign, perhaps fearing that dwelling on it in any further detail risked somehow emptying his reservoir of motivation for good.

As the author wrote in the *Autocourse* annual: "It must be heartbreaking to see your career evaporating in front of your eyes… If Honda can't deliver in '08, then he needs to bail out and find another berth. He not only needs better, but needs it urgently."

For the moment, however, it was just a case of reeling off the balance of the 2007 calendar and hoping that things would be different in 2008, although quite why this seemed a very likely prospect was difficult to see.

Jenson leads Nick Heidfeld's BMW-Sauber, despite the loss of his front wing in a previous skirmish with the German, during the 2007 Japanese Grand Prix at Fuji. Jenson eventually retired after a collision with Takuma Sato's Super Aguri.
📷 LAT

Jenson always tried to look on the bright side, even though a rather cheeky sense of the ironic would emerge from time to time. The race at the Hungaroring resulted in another retirement for him due to a throttle sensor problem, while Rubens finished in 18th and last place.

At Istanbul Park for the Turkish Grand Prix both Hondas had to start from the back of the grid after they required post-qualifying engine changes. Barrichello was up to 18th by the end of the opening lap, but gradually Jenson hauled him in to the point where a radio message to Rubens went out instructing him to allow Jenson past because he felt he was quicker. Rubens's response was a quite understandable: "You've gotta be kidding me!"

Yet Button got through to 13th, four places ahead of the Brazilian, by the time they reached the chequered flag. By his own admission he got involved in a number of enjoyable scraps. "It was a lot of fun passing ten cars," said Jenson. "If you put to one side where we finished – because 13th is still a far from good result – I think we had a reasonable race compared with the last one."

Yet if you glanced at the Drivers' World Championship table after the Turkish race, particularly knowing what we

eventually the clutch began slipping, the power steering packed up and he eventually had to stop seven laps from the finish with hydraulic failure.

Honda was obviously hoping for a morale-boosting result in the Japanese Grand Prix, particularly in view of the fact that the race was being staged at the Toyota-owned Mount Fuji track. Jenson qualified sixth in conditions of light rain, an excellent showing. After the wet race started behind the safety car, and both Ferraris had made two stops (to change to extreme-wet tyres and then to refuel), he was up to fourth when the safety car was withdrawn for the first time after 19 laps. Unfortunately, he lost his front wing in a skirmish with Nick Heidfeld's BMW Sauber, but continued without it until his scheduled stop on lap 23, only to be further delayed by a throttle problem. He overtook Barrichello for 11th, then collided with Takuma Sato's Super Aguri and failed to make it to the finish.

There were now two races to go, China and Brazil. In China, while the eyes of the world's media were firmly focused over whether or not Lewis Hamilton would storm to the World Championship title in his first year of F1 competition, Jenson achieved his most productive result of the year with a fifth-place finish between the Toro Rossos of Vettel and Vitantonio Liuzzi.

"It was a fantastic race today and I'm very happy to come away with four points and our best result of the season," said Button. "I struggled at the start because the car was not working well in the wet conditions and I had no grip, so I ended up slipping back. When the track dried out we decided to go for the dry option tyre and a light fuel load."

Hydraulics failure brought to an end Jenson's drive in the season-ending Brazilian Grand Prix. He was 15th in the World Championship on just 6 points. Not good, by any manner or means. Things could only get better. But where had we heard that before?

← **Letting off steam. Off-duty on a night out in London with Rick Parfitt Jnr.**
Rex Features

know now, there was a certain poignancy. In 16th and 17th places, on a single point apiece, were new boy Sebastian Vettel and Jenson. On the basis of what we had seen so far in 2007, one might well have characterised them as ships that pass in the night, one climbing the lower rungs of the F1 ladder as a wide-eyed aspirant, the other trying to save a career that was in danger of going into free-fall.

Who could possibly have imagined that, just 24 months later, these same two men would be eyeball-to-eyeball for the 2009 title crown?

That low-points parity disappeared at Monza, where Jenson came from tenth on the grid to finish eighth – immediately doubling his points tally to date. "It was nice to get a point today," he admitted; "but it was a frustrating race for me as I had so much understeer on my first stint.

"We run such low front wing around this circuit that it is very easy to lock the front tyres, particularly at Parabolica, and I flat-spotted the right front tyre which meant I was losing grip through every right-hander.

"This meant that I was not able to fend off Nico Rosberg [who eventually finished sixth], but the team had done a great job and everyone is in good spirits, so I'm pleased to have got another point for them. They really deserve it."

As expected, the Honda team struggled at Spa-Francorchamps where the high-speed swerves really highlighted the car's aerodynamic shortcomings. As usual, Jenson drove its wheels off, battling hard as it yawed between understeer and oversteer throughout the lap, but

"IT WAS A LOT OF FUN PASSING TEN CARS. IF YOU PUT TO ONE SIDE WHERE WE FINISHED – BECAUSE 13TH IS STILL A FAR FROM GOOD RESULT – I THINK WE HAD A REASONABLE RACE…"
JENSON BUTTON

are as good as anyone. Let's hope we can give them the material to do the job."

Netting Brawn represented a huge coup for Honda, whose Chief Executive Nick Fry admitted he had spent the previous seven months trying to finalise a deal which could be the most important in the team's history so far. After masterminding Michael Schumacher's five consecutive World Championships at Ferrari between 2000 and 2004, Brawn decided to take a year's sabbatical after Schumacher retired at the end of 2006.

Despite this, it was always felt within the F1 community that he would return to Ferrari in 2007, but with Jean Todt remaining in the role of overall Chief Executive for the famous Italian company, Brawn concluded that the challenge of returning to his old haunts in Italy would be "like putting on a very comfortable glove."

Although he retained cordial links with Ferrari, and agreed to talk to them first when he decided to consider a return to F1, eventually the fact that he had been living back in the UK for the past 12 months, helped incline him towards accepting the Honda job. Accordingly, Ferrari confirmed that his protégé, the former Sporting Director Stefano Domenicali, would be promoted to chief of the company's racing department

"The fact that Ferrari wasn't in crisis made it less attractive to me," said Brawn. "They've done well and will do well, and have got a good structure there to go forward with. My job now is to beat them."

Reflecting on his sabbatical, he added: "The 12 months away helped me focus a bit on what I enjoyed about racing, what aspects I enjoy. I miss the racing a lot. I miss the sport, I miss the teamwork, I miss being a part of a group of people who achieve something that is very difficult, but when achieved is very rewarding. I had a wonderful year but you can only indulge yourself for so long."

In his new role, Brawn would assume full responsibility for designing, manufacturing, engineering and racing Honda's F1 car. Ross would work alongside Nick Fry, who continued as Chief Executive of the team.

Brawn refused to put any sort of time limit on how long it might take the team to achieve success, making the point that he only visited the Honda F1 headquarters at Brackley over the last few days, as he did not want to fuel speculation about his possible plans before he had finally reached a firm agreement.

"I think the [Honda] facilities are top class, as good as anyone [in the business]," he said. "In terms of the top level of F1, Honda are closer to it than Ferrari was when I joined 10 years ago."

Button, who had won just a single race in 135 starts, was left be hoping he was right.

↑ Jenson walks the paddock with new Honda Team Principal Ross Brawn at the 2008 Bahrain Grand Prix.
📷 LAT

↗ Jenson loses his front wing after tangling with Nick Heidfeld at Monaco in 2008.
📷 LAT

Three weeks later, the Brackley-based F1 team received a huge boost when it was announced that Ross Brawn, the former Ferrari Technical Director, had been appointed Team Principal of the Honda F1 operation. And he kicked off by stating publicly it was his view that Jenson and Rubens were both outstanding drivers and fully capable of scoring grands prix victories for the Honda team once they were both given the right equipment.

"My view is that both the team's drivers are more than capable," said Brawn, who reputedly signed a performance-related contract which could deliver him as much as $6m a year if the team started to achieve hard results. "The drivers are not an issue. On his day Rubens was as quick as Michael [Schumacher] and Jenson is outstanding. They

Yet the initial signs would not be good. Button's hopes of returning to the F1 winners' circle and adding to his single Grand Prix victory so far looked as though they were going to be frustrated by the disappointing initial form displayed by the new Honda RA108 during early testing in preparation for the season-opening Australian Grand Prix.

Button made clear his disappointment after the three days' testing at Barcelona's Circuit de Catalunya. He did, however, make it clear that he was "pleased with the reliability of the car," F1 code for 'but the damn' thing's not quick enough.'

This was clearly a huge disappointment not only for Button, but also a setback for Ross Brawn, who had hoped that the 2008 car would offer a stable technical base on

"MY VIEW IS THAT BOTH THE TEAM'S DRIVERS ARE MORE THAN CAPABLE. THE DRIVERS ARE NOT AN ISSUE. ON HIS DAY RUBENS WAS AS QUICK AS MICHAEL [SCHUMACHER] AND JENSON IS OUTSTANDING"

ROSS BRAWN

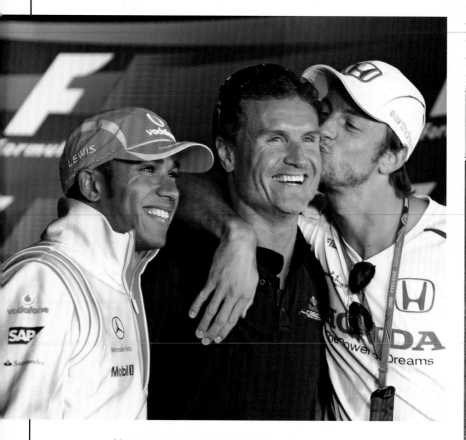

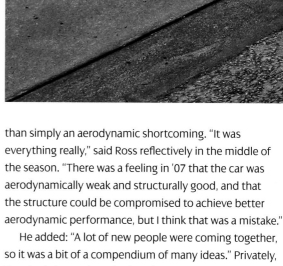

> ## "THERE WAS A FEELING IN '07 THAT THE CAR WAS AERODYNAMICALLY WEAK AND STRUCTURALLY GOOD… BUT I THINK THAT WAS A MISTAKE"
>
> **ROSS BRAWN**

↑ **Silverstone 2008. Jenson and Lewis Hamilton help David Coulthard to announce his retirement from F1.**
📷 LAT

↗ **Another mediocre race to 13th in the 2008 European Grand Prix at Valencia.**
📷 Getty Images

which to build a winning package for 2009, but now it seemed that it was a case of back to basics.

Somehow, the controversial 'earth dreams' livery which had been adopted for the new season – intended to flag up Honda's commitment to environmentally friendly technical solutions – also became an unnecessarily irksome dead weight around the team's neck. Had the cars been competitive and achieving worthwhile results, such free-thinking might have been accepted as a positive message. As it was, it just seemed to send a subliminal message that Honda was all superficial presentation and no worthwhile substance.

It did not take Brawn long to appreciate that the problems with the Honda RA108 ran somewhat deeper

than simply an aerodynamic shortcoming. "It was everything really," said Ross reflectively in the middle of the season. "There was a feeling in '07 that the car was aerodynamically weak and structurally good, and that the structure could be compromised to achieve better aerodynamic performance, but I think that was a mistake."

He added: "A lot of new people were coming together, so it was a bit of a compendium of many ideas." Privately, Ross had always thought that the 2008 season would turn out to be one in which the foundations for future success would be laid. Looking back on how events unfolded, he could never have imagined precisely how dramatically prescient this strategy would be. Results, of which there would be precious few, would be regarded as a bonus.

Melbourne, the first race, set the tone for Jenson's season. He clipped Sebastian Vettel's Toro Rosso at the first corner, and was one of five drivers to go clattering into the barrier when the race was only a few seconds old. Oh yes, and Rubens was disqualified after leaving the pit lane against a red light.

Tenth place in Malaysia was nothing to write home about, then Bahrain delivered another collision with David Coulthard's Red Bull for the second straight year. "I guess it was me who hit him," shrugged Jenson, "but I'd assumed he would stay where he was."

In Spain, the Honda RA108 looked a little more convincing. Jenson had a busy race which involved queuing behind Rubens awaiting his pit stop, and

brushing wheels with Giancarlo Fisichella as they left the pit lane.

"The car's rear end was a bit twitchy at first," said Button, "but the balance was very good during the middle stint, once the track rubbered in." Shortly before the finish he set fifth-fastest lap of the race "just to see what the car could do." Still, it was good to have three championship points on the board.

A painful trawl through Jenson's remaining races of the year can be taken by referring to the results sequence at the back of this book. In the final race of the year, the Brazilian Grand Prix at Interlagos, Jenson could only limp home 13th. To say his progress was unnoticed would be a gross understatement. This, after all, was the day on

↑**Up in smoke.
Jenson's 2008
season was
summed up when
his Honda caught
fire at the end of
the season-closing
Brazilian Grand
Prix at Interlagos.**
📷 sutton-images.com

which Lewis Hamilton snatched the World Championship on the very last lap by a single point from Felipe Massa. Lewis had 98 points on the board. Jenson still had the three he'd scored at Barcelona. He was 18th and last in the drivers' rankings.

The Brazilian Grand Prix took place on November 2nd. A month later the UK motor racing press was invited to the team's customary end-of-season lunch at Raymond Blanc's luxury five-star restaurant, 'Le Manoir aux Quatres Saisons', near Oxford. A couple of days before this fixture – so obviously, on reflection, dramatically out of step with the troubled times in F1, it was cancelled.

There was worse news to come. On the morning of December 4th it was confirmed from Tokyo that Honda

would close down their F1 team before the start of the 2009 season, unless a buyer could be found for the operation which employed over 700 people at their factory at Brackley, Northamptonshire.

The news, which had obviously seismic implications for the sport's future, looked as though it would leave Jenson Button out of a drive for 2009, and destroy any prospect of Bruno Senna, the nephew of the late Ayrton Senna and a likely replacement for Rubens Barrichello, graduating to the sport's senior category as the British driver's team-mate.

Button, who won the team's only Grand Prix victory of the contemporary era, seemed likely to find it difficult to find an opening elsewhere, as all the top teams had already finalised their driver line-ups for 2009. Prior to Button's victory in Budapest, Honda had only scored two grands prix victories as a constructor, in Mexico with Richie Ginther in 1965, and at Monza with John Surtees two years later.

More worryingly, Honda's decision threatened far-reaching implications for a sport which has all too-often considered itself immune from the commercial turbulence of the economic market place, triggering fears that Toyota, who have been competing in F1 at huge expense and with little success since 2002, could follow Honda's example and quit the sport.

The other F1 teams were told of Honda's decision at a meeting of the Formula One Teams Association (FOTA) in London on December 10th, and the workforce was told that they would be on three months' notice as from the start of January 2010.

"They [Honda] have a month to find a buyer, otherwise they are closing the team," one highly placed source quoted Honda team bosses Ross Brawn and Nick Fry as telling that meeting.

"It's very, very sad for Formula One to see a team with the heritage of Honda leaving the sport," said the source,

adding it was no real surprise given the team "were running up costs to a level that were self-evidently unsustainable."

Furthermore, Honda's withdrawal risked the possibility that there might only be 18 cars on the World Championship starting grids in 2009, and may have prompted several other teams to rethink whether F1 was worth the investment in the current climate. Others felt that Honda's decision was simply a direct result of the fact that the team had consistently under-delivered in terms of hard results in recent years.

Now it seemed that Ross Brawn would have to deploy all his skill and negotiating nous to find a potential buyer for the team who could commit to bankrolling the £200m annual cost of running such an operation, perhaps using the supply of Ferrari 'customer' engines made available by the Force India team's recent decision to switch to Mercedes power for 2009.

Overwhelmingly, Honda's decision to quit would give added impetus to a package of cost-cutting measures which were due to be submitted to the FIA World Motorsport Council a few days later. Welcome and long overdue, perhaps, but possibly too late to save Honda.

Or was it?

⬇ Jenson's car may be burning, but he still finds time to congratulate Lewis Hamilton on winning the 2008 World Drivers' Championship on the nail-biting final lap in Brazil.
📷 LAT

[09]

2009 – FROM ZERO TO HERO

It was almost as if the F1 community as a whole had been winded by a punch in the belly. The immediate implications for the Honda team were simply devastating, as indeed were the prospects for their suppliers in the Brackley area, that close-knit community of motorsport sub-contractors in the Northamptonshire countryside just north of Oxford. Somehow it seemed just too much to imagine that a major F1 competitor was about to be taken out of business by the commercial realities of a wider world, from which optimists had misguidedly believed their high-octane business was magically insulated.

It was one of the most painful wake-up calls for the World Championship in a couple of decades. A chill wind indeed ran down the pit lane like a thin dog. The immediate problem might only have impinged with dramatic immediacy on the Honda workforce, but everywhere else in the F1 business the same question was being nervously articulated: "Who next?"

On Friday December 5th, the official announcement of the decision was made by Honda's President and CEO, Takeo Fukui. Following a night of frenzied and distracted speculation over the F1 team's future, Fukui announced at a hastily convened press conference in Tokyo that difficult financial conditions had left the car maker with no alternative but to make the much-feared decision.

"Honda must protect its core business activities and secure the long term, as widespread uncertainties in the economies around the globe continue to mount," he said. "A recovery is expected to take some time.

"Under these circumstances, Honda has taken swift and flexible measures to counter this sudden and expansive weakening of the marketplace in all business areas.

"However, in recognition of the need to optimize the allocation of management resources, including investment regarding the future, we have decided to withdraw from Formula 1 participation.

"We will enter into consultation with the associates of Honda Racing F1 Team and its engine supplier Honda Racing Development regarding the future of the two companies. This will include offering the team for sale."

In reality, it became extremely clear in a matter of days that whoever took over the team would not be afforded the luxury of using Honda engines. Almost the first thing that Honda did after they made the announcement was to gather up all the Honda V8s which remained at Brackley and transport them to HRD's premises at Bracknell, about 40 miles away. There was a touch of symbolism – arguably even paranoia – about the seeming urgency behind this move.

Over the following weekend, team principal Ross Brawn and CEO Nick Fry flew to Tokyo for urgent talks with their Japanese chiefs about the future, to examine whether there was any chance of romancing the Honda board into

← **The future looks bright as Jenson gives the thumbs-up in Bahrain, after a fairytale start to the 2009 season with Brawn GP.**
📷 LAT

↑ **Ross Brawn and Rubens Barrichello listen eagerly to Jenson's opinion on the Brawn BGP001, after his first laps in the car during testing at Silverstone on 6 March 2009.**
📷 LAT

changing its mind, or, failing that, ascertaining precisely how the sale of the company would be arranged.

Even at this early stage, a plan was beginning to develop in Brawn's mind, although it would take some honing and development before it came to fruition. The team would only be funded until March 2009, and its 700-plus workforce would be under formal notice from the start of January.

Fukui confessed that the withdrawal decision had been a hard one to take, particularly in view of the fact that Honda had scored Button's memorable victory in Hungary over two years earlier, and had already invested a huge amount of money in bidding to return to the top under the leadership of Brawn.

He commented: "In its third era of Formula One

activities, Honda has been participating in Formula One races from the 2000 season, initially with BAR, by adopting a new format of jointly developing racing machines. Subsequently, in a move to meet the changing environment surrounding Formula One, we switched to running a 100% Honda-owned team commencing with the 2006 season.

"Surmounting many challenges, the Honda Team achieved a Grand Prix victory in 2006, enabling Honda to receive overwhelming support from Honda fans around the world that were looking forward to greater success.

"It, therefore, has been an extremely difficult decision for us to come to this conclusion without having been able to fully meet the expectations of our fans.

"By making the best of what we have learned during these times of economic turmoil, coupled with the spirit of challenge gained through active participation in racing, we intend to continue with our commitment in meeting new challenges.

"Finally, we would like to take this opportunity to sincerely thank our fans and all those who have supported Honda's Formula One efforts, including everyone in the world of Formula One." Touching words, perhaps, but of little hard or practical use to the Honda personnel and drivers who were now staring into the abyss. And ironic, had they not been so painful, coming as they did only 12 months after Honda had persuaded Ross that theirs was the team for him.

As for Jenson, it looked as though it might be the end of the F1 road. He had an admittedly lucrative, long-term contract with Honda in place for an unspecified term, but there was talk that he could earn in excess of $30m over the next three years. Clearly Honda could not walk away from such a commitment without compensating the British driver, but it was clear that he would have to compromise. And he would clearly also have to compromise if a new owner came in and he decided to stay with them. And, to be frank, there were not too many vacant slots available for him to consider.

Button had now been in F1 for nine seasons. Amazingly, there were too many people in the pit lane who still had him subliminally tagged as 'playboy' or 'insufficiently committed.' Yet, in truth, not many people in the know thought that was the case. F1 personalities who knew about that of which they spoke, like Jackie Stewart or Niki Lauda, held him in the highest regard. They could see past his short-term potential to fully appreciate his core value.

It was in early December that speculation of a potential career lifeline was raised, when reports began to circulate that there might be some interest in Jenson's services from Scuderia Toro Rosso, one of the few teams to then still have a vacant slot left for 2009.

Franz Tost, the Toro Rosso team principal, was known to have a high opinion of the 28-year-old British driver, having worked with him when he drove for the Williams-BMW squad during his F1 debut season in 2000.

Sources close to the Faenza-based team speculated that Button could be invited by Tost to test one of their STR02s, similar to that in which Sebastian Vettel won the rain-soaked Italian Grand Prix at Monza in September, at the three-day test session scheduled for Spain's Jerez circuit from December 10th–12th. But Button would not comment on the issue and it never happened.

As the days ticked off towards the first race of the season in Melbourne, so it seemed as though Ross Brawn's rescue attempt was edging ever closer. It was going to be a damn' close run thing, but by the end of February 2009 all the parties were going through the process of submitting all the necessary paperwork and documentation to Companies House.

The bid to save Honda received a welcome boost when Frank Williams and his company's Chief Executive Adam Parr said they expected the team to be ready to compete in Australia. Williams said: "They're a bunch of racers who I admire very much, so yes, they might make it."

Parr added: "I think they'll make it. The fact that they're still talking is quite instrumental. If the Honda parent company wasn't faced with any serious opportunity, then I think they'd have just called it a day, wouldn't they?

"The fact that we're four weeks away from the beginning of the season and they're still making kit must mean that Honda takes the proposals that are available very seriously."

In the end, it all came together, and Jenson Button gave the new Mercedes-engined Brawn BGP001 its preliminary shakedown at Silverstone only hours after it was announced that Ross Brawn had purchased the Brackley-based team from its Japanese owners. No figures were made public, but it was widely speculated that Ross had successfully persuaded the Japanese car company to invest the $50m or so they would have had to outlay on redundancy payments and lease termination fees on actually keeping the team going for a year. So Brawn GP was effectively being given a financial flying start. It was gratifying, sure enough, but they went into the deal knowing that they would be on their own in 2010.

Button and Barrichello were highly impressed with the Mercedes V8. It was strong, had a lusty power band and plenty of punch. It compared so favourably with the Honda V8 that it was almost an embarrassment. Rubens muttered: "I've been waiting for this car for such a long time. In a way

"THE FACT THAT WE'RE FOUR WEEKS AWAY FROM THE BEGINNING OF THE SEASON AND THEY'RE STILL MAKING KIT MUST MEAN THAT HONDA TAKES THE PROPOSALS THAT ARE AVAILABLE VERY SERIOUSLY"

ADAM PARR

I have waited for it since I joined Honda, to have a car that can give me that good feeling.

"Every race last year I went in to win. It was a tough time. But now the car is competitive and although the team changed name, we've learned."

Jenson just grinned broadly in agreement: "The car's speed blew my mind," he said. "I could feel every bump, and I could do so much with it because it did the same thing every time I hit the brakes. It was consistent and reliable, and just incredibly fast."

There was no trouble getting agreement from the other teams to change the name from Honda to Brawn. The successful sale of the Honda team was a development which prompted a collective sigh of relief across the entire F1 community. At a time when the global motor industry had been besieged by economic setbacks, the news that a major player of Honda's calibre was hell-bent on scrapping its Formula One programme might have been understandable, but it was also deeply depressing for the sport which prided itself on being the best possible calling card for car makers across the world.

It had briefly been thought that the team might be

renamed Tyrrell. After all, BAR sprang from the flickering embers of the famous Surrey-based team which had carried Jackie Stewart to his three World Championships in 1969, '71 and '73. But when Ross and his fellow directors sat and discussed the matter with their marketing people they reached the conclusion that 'Tyrrell' belonged to yesteryear.

"It was decided that the name did not identify with the present generation of fans and sponsors," said Ross. "So we decided that the team's name should have a more contemporary title." Brawn it was.

Even so, Ross conceded that the new organisation had something of a buccaneering appeal to it, redolent of an earlier generation. "We're in a slightly odd position because the car was born with the resources of a big team and is now being raced with the resources of a small team," he told Bradley Lord of *F1 Racing* magazine.

"The retro-element of the team – the smallness, the fact that it carries the team principal's name, like Williams or Jordan – seems to have been taken on very enthusiastically by the public."

Brawn had proved that all was not doom and gloom in

Jenson behind the wheel of the Brawn BGP001 for the first time at the car's debut Silverstone test.

LAT

"THE CAR'S SPEED BLEW MY MIND… I COULD FEEL EVERY BUMP, AND I COULD DO SO MUCH WITH IT BECAUSE IT DID THE SAME THING EVERY TIME I HIT THE BRAKES. IT WAS CONSISTENT AND RELIABLE, AND JUST INCREDIBLY FAST"

JENSON BUTTON

Formula One by guaranteeing that there would now be 20 cars on the grid in Australia rather than the 18 there would have been had Honda proceeded with its plans to close the team. And 18 cars would have been uncomfortably close to the minimum of 16 which Bernie Ecclestone, the sport's commercial rights holder, was contracted to supply for each Grand Prix.

Ross commented: "The past few months have been extremely challenging for the team, but today's announcement is the very pleasing conclusion to the strenuous efforts that have been made to secure its future.

"Firstly, it is a great shame that having worked with Honda Motor Company for so long we can no longer continue together. I would like to thank Honda for the fantastic co-operation and support we have received throughout this process – particularly those members of the senior management who were closely involved with concluding our agreement – and for the faith they have demonstrated in myself and our team.

"I would also like to take this opportunity to pay due credit to our staff at Brackley. The levels of motivation and commitment that I have witnessed at the factory deserve the highest praise.

"I am delighted that Jenson and Rubens will form our race driver line-up for the 2009 season. The vast experience and knowledge that both drivers bring to our team will prove invaluable as we aim to get up to speed in the shortest possible time to be ready for the first race of the season in Melbourne on March 29th. In what will be their fourth season together, their experience with our team in Brackley, our systems and our engineers, will prove a real asset."

The team was scaled down, with 270 of the workforce being made redundant. Instead of between 90 and 100 staff attending the races, this would be pared down to just under 50. Button took a large pay cut which was estimated to be around two-thirds of his agreed income.

Button had been unbelievably impressed with his first taste of the Brawn BGP001, stunned even. That really should not have been too much of a surprise. The car's

technical development, driven by Brawn, was effectively kick-started in the closing months of 2007. If the pit lane gossip was to be believed, the Brawn BGP001 benefited from the services of no fewer than four wind tunnels during its evolutionary phase. "That's about twice as much as expended at McLaren," said a highly placed personality in the Woking team. Again, it made you think.

Yet there was a potential snag on the horizon. In the run-up to the opening race of the 2009 season in Melbourne, a question mark arose over several teams' interpretation of the aerodynamic regulations, specifically

The Brawn's controversial 'double diffuser' can be clearly seen in this view of the rear of the car. The central opening, below the rain light, was the sticking point.

sutton-images.com

"THEY ARE MAKING THE REST OF US LOOK LIKE AMATEURS… IN AUSTRALIA THEY WILL DISAPPEAR ON THE BASIS OF WHAT WE HAVE SEEN IN TESTING. I JUST HOPE WE CAN BE UP THERE TOO"

FRANK WILLIAMS

whether or not the so-called 'double diffuser' adopted by Brawn, Williams and Toyota was strictly legal.

Thus the new season began under a cloud, with several teams poised to lodge a protest over the eligibility of the 'double diffuser' cars when they were presented for scrutineering at the Albert Park circuit.

Meanwhile, veteran Formula One team principal Sir Frank Williams fuelled the frenzied speculation about the potential of the Brawn squad by predicting there was a very real likelihood of Jenson Button or Rubens Barrichello dominating the first race.

Williams, whose cars last won a Grand Prix with Juan Pablo Montoya in Brazil five years ago, admitted that he thought that the Brawn team's impressive pace in pre-season testing, where they had made fools of the rest of the field, was an accurate reflection of their genuine promise.

"They are making the rest of us look like amateurs," Williams said. "In Australia they will disappear on the basis of what we have seen in testing. I just hope we can be up there too."

Fernando Alonso, twice winner of the World Championship in 2005 and '06, echoed Williams's sentiments.

"The times set by the Brawn cars in testing are impressive and suggest they will be racing at the front in Melbourne," Alonso told the *Herald Sun* newspaper in Melbourne. "However, testing is one thing and racing is another, and as with our other competitors there could be some surprises this year."

He added: "Obviously the performance of Brawn GP is a big surprise for everyone and I think they will be strong. McLaren have not looked so competitive recently, but until we get to Melbourne we won't know how the teams really

compare, as you should never read too much into testing times. I wouldn't want to underestimate any of our rivals."

Almost on the eve of the Australian Grand Prix, Brawn cemented a sponsorship deal with Richard Branson's Virgin group, and the colourful entrepreneur duly turned up in the paddock at Albert Park. According to reports, the personal relationship between Jenson and Branson got off on a rather tense note; Branson was much taken with Button's girlfriend, Jessica, and at one point had to be told to back off in quite direct terms. It made for a rather delicate atmosphere.

In qualifying and the race it proved to be a Brawn grand slam, just as Frank Williams had predicted. And, as Peter Windsor wrote perceptively in *F1 Racing* magazine, all Jenson really had to do was harness his impeccable driving technique to keep the car away from the unyielding barriers which always seem so claustrophobically close at Melbourne.

Button admitted that the late completion of his new car meant he was a bit rusty, but it was nothing that was insurmountable. "I let the tyres get too cold behind the safety car [caused by a shunt involving Kazuki Nakajima's Williams] and I flat-spotted them at the restart. That was

→ **Jenson's girlfriend, Jessica Michibata, was at his side for much of the 2009 season.**
📷 Rex Features

↑ Leading the field away from a dominant pole position at the opening race of the 2009 season in Australia.
📷 LAT

← After the uncertainty surrounding their future at the start of the year, Jenson and Rubens celebrate a remarkable 1–2 finish on the podium at Melbourne.
📷 LAT

↑ **Jenson surfs towards victory in the rain-soaked Malaysian Grand Prix at Sepang.**
📷 LAT

↓ **Two wins in seven days – the smiles say it all.**
📷 LAT

silly. Then I overshot my second pit stop and had the thing in the wrong gear. But that's just lack of driving. It's something to work on for Malaysia."

Button let out the rope in a disciplined fashion, allowing Barrichello to close up to just 0.807sec behind as the two white Brawns took the chequered flag pretty much as an eight wheeler. It couldn't get much better than this. Or could it?

Jenson and the Brawn-Mercedes had only just scratched the surface of their potential. A week later Jenson boosted his Grand Prix victory tally to three – and two in seven days – when he surfed past the chequered flag at Sepang, in the Malaysian Grand Prix. The race was red-flagged to a halt when a torrential tropical thunderstorm left the track virtually flooded, with conditions unmanageable even at a little more than walking pace.

Button's success was rewarded with only half the customary allocation of championship points, as the event had been stopped with 26 of its original 56 laps to run, thus not reaching the two-thirds cut-off point beyond which full points are awarded. Button now led the championship with 15 points, well ahead of Barrichello.

Second place fell to Nick Heidfeld's BMW Sauber, ahead of Timo Glock in the Toyota. Button said that, in the few laps before the race was flagged to a halt, the weather was so bad that he could not keep up with the Mercedes safety car, which had been deployed to slow the field.

"That was so embarrassing," he said. "We were going at walking pace and really I thought I could run round faster. The team in the pits were telling me all I had to do was drive round. The visibility was so bad that it was impossible to see the circuit."

The dramatic race, which sorely taxed the virtuoso driving skills of the world's top drivers, was the first for 18 years to be flagged to a halt due to heavy rain. The previous GP to suffer such a fate was the 1991 Australian Grand Prix at Adelaide, which was abandoned after barely a dozen laps when Nigel Mansell crashed his Williams in pursuit of Ayrton Senna's winning McLaren-Honda.

It was all rather a stark contrast to the humid and torrid conditions in which the battle for grid positions was fought out. Button was well in control, retaining his composure and control to qualify on pole position by one-tenth of a second. With five minutes of the session left to go, it seemed as though Rubens Barrichello might join his Brawn team-mate on the front row of the grid, but late spurts by Jarno Trulli's Toyota and Sebastian Vettel's Red Bull pushed him down to fourth. Unfortunately for Rubens, he was then demoted a further five places due to a gearbox change after Friday practice.

However, Jenson was fully aware that he would have to handle a strong challenge from Ferrari drivers Felipe Massa and Kimi Räikkönen, on a circuit where his Brawn-Mercedes's impressive traction exiting slow and medium speed corners yielded less of performance advantage than was the case at Melbourne's Albert Park circuit.

"I think we have a lot more competition this weekend than we had in Australia," said Button. "I think Ferrari, despite their problems in Australia, and Red Bull, will be very hard to beat." He was right as far as Red Bull was concerned, with Vettel, but the Ferraris were still hobbled by handling problems and could not deliver their hoped-for improvement. Come the race, however, the weather made most of the predictions academic.

In the break between the second and third races of the season, the senior personnel of the F1 teams caught up in the 'double diffuser' controversy returned to Europe to continue their argument in front of the FIA Court of Appeal. Here, they would determine once and for all the legality of such technical accessories.

Protests against these diffuser designs were lodged at Melbourne by the Ferrari, Red Bull and Renault teams. Since the Australian race, both the BMW Sauber and McLaren squads had indicated that they would also be attending the hearing.

The effect of the controversial 'double diffuser' design was to offer more grip to the cars concerned, improving their traction, particularly out of tight corners, and thereby exerting a performance edge over those cars equipped with 'conventional' diffusers.

Ferrari design consultant Rory Byrne, who was a close friend and colleague of Ross Brawn during their time together working for the Maranello team, offered his view

More wet weather for the Chinese Grand Prix, where the Red Bulls had the measure of the Brawns, but Jenson still finished on the podium in third place.
📷 LAT

that the three teams concerned had broken with a 15-year protocol over how the aerodynamic rules were interpreted.

"Ross Brawn and I remain good friends," Byrne was quick to insist. "But one thing is personal relationships, another is the professional aspect. And I work for Ferrari."

However, Patrick Head, the director and co-owner of the William team, said he was absolutely satisfied that the interpretation permitting the so-called 'double diffuser' was consistent with both the intention of the regulations and the meaning of the wording. Either way, the Court of Appeal meeting certainly turned into a very turbulent forum.

Ferrari's lawyer, Nigel Tozzi, opened his address to the court by describing Brawn as a "person of supreme arrogance," an observation which brought wry smiles to the faces of many who recalled that the British engineer was the key technical driving force behind the five World Championship titles which Michael Schumacher won with the famous Italian team.

Tozzi eventually concluded his 90-minute opening address by returning to the same theme. "Only a person of supreme arrogance would think he is right when so many of his esteemed colleagues would disagree," he said of Brawn.

The arcane technical arguments relating to the legality of the diffusers centred round the positioning of certain apertures in the undertrays of the cars in question. Tozzi railed: "Anyone with a command of English will tell you it's a hole, so do not let someone attempting to be clever with words defeat the express purpose of the rules."

He added: "The appeal is not because we have not made the most of an opportunity, but because Brawn, Toyota and Williams have not acted within the regulations." That was as maybe, but the fact of the matter was that the FIA Court of Appeal adjudged the Brawn to be legal, so the dissenting teams climbed aboard the long flight to Shanghai for the Chinese Grand Prix knowing that, having failed to despatch it, they now had to match it.

Back in Shanghai, the weather conditions played brilliantly into the hands of the Red Bulls, with Sebastian Vettel delivering a repeat of the wet-weather brilliance which had seen him deliver victory so majestically for the Toro Rosso team the previous year at Monza. Mark Webber finished second, the best result of his career so far, which he achieved by pulling a brilliant overtaking move on Button's Brawn, consigning the World Championship leader to the third step of the rostrum.

⬇ **Battling with Lewis Hamilton during the opening lap of the Bahrain Grand Prix. Jenson passed Lewis's KERS-equipped McLaren in a decisive move at the end of the pit straight.**

📷 LAT

The trouble with starting a season with a couple of wins straight off the bat is that if you don't continually duplicate those high standards, the perception is that you are a disappointment. Jenson and his team-mate were hostages to just that sort of misfortune at Shanghai.

Both Brawns began the race carrying a lot of fuel, so had it been a dry and undramatic event, it is likely they would have been even closer to the Red Bulls than proved to be the case in the rain. Both Jenson and Rubens complained of problems getting their tyres up to operating temperature in the sodden conditions, so third and fourth places was pretty good.

"I felt like I was really slow," Button said, "because I was trying to miss every river, but the problem with that is that the circuit conditions are changing every lap and the position of the rivers is constantly moving. When I saw that Mark and I were pulling away from the people behind, I was reasonably happy and just sort of settled into a pace."

It was in China that Flavio Briatore, the Renault team principal, referred scathingly to the Brawn team, saying that their early-season supremacy was damaging the image of F1.

Speaking to a group of Italian journalists, he said that neither of the Brawn drivers was of sufficiently high calibre to be regarded as a World Championship contender.

"The drivers in our team have been and are World Champions," he said testily, "and yet the title is (this year) being fought out between one driver who is a semi-pensioner and another who is a decent bloke, but like a roadside post."

Jenson brushed the remarks aside, saying it was just a sign of bitterness: "He also needs to remember that he tried to employ me for this year."

If anybody thought that perhaps Shanghai revealed the first signs of wobbling on Button's part, they were to be mistaken. Bahrain was next on the calendar, and Jenson responded to the tricky, sand-blasted track conditions with great composure, to score his third win out of four races.

It was one of those defining performances, where a competitor simply radiates self-belief to the point where he mentally steps up a gear almost without realising it. There was a tangible frisson of crackling on-top-of-the-job confidence about the British driver's entire demeanour, a mood which sent the unmistakable message "you might not have thought I was capable of this, but I never doubted it for a second."

⬇ **Back on top of his game. Jenson takes the chequered flag to win in Bahrain.**
📷 LAT

"WE KNEW THAT MASSA WAS HEAVY AND THE LAST THING I NEEDED WAS TO BE STUCK BEHIND HIM AFTER MY PIT STOP. I WANTED TO OPEN A GAP. I WANTED RUBENS TO PICK UP THE PACE"

JENSON BUTTON

It's been noticed – and indeed noted – by the great and the good, on many occasions, just how much like Michael Schumacher Jenson is when you see his steering input from the in-car camera. The Brawn-Mercedes simply shimmered from apex to apex at the Sakhir circuit, Button almost willing the car to change direction rather than using great lashings of lock and sawing away at the wheel.

The key to it all was Jenson's opening two laps. From fourth on the grid, Jenson passed Sebastian Vettel's Red Bull on the inside of the second turn, before slipstreaming Lewis Hamilton's fast-starting McLaren and outbraking him as they went into turn one on the second occasion. This allowed the Brawn driver to run third in the opening stages, behind the Toyotas of Timo Glock and Trulli, who were both running light cars scheduled for early pit stops. But the way the tactical cards fell meant that Jarno Trulli certainly played a key role. When Jenson made his first pit stop, after three super-quick laps leading in clear air, Sebastian Vettel went through into the lead. But, after making his pit stop, the Red Bull driver resumed behind Trulli, who was struggling with his second set of tyres. By this time, Jenson was 7sec ahead of Trulli, and the crucial cushion was in place. And, of course, Jenson never put a wheel wrong.

Back to Europe, and Jenson bagged a commanding pole position for the Spanish Grand Prix at Barcelona, ahead of Vettel's Red Bull and Barrichello in the other Brawn. Rubens burst through from the second row to lead into the first corner, and the Brazilian controlled the race in the opening stages, although by lap nine of the race Jenson was thinking: "Come on Rubens, you can go quicker than this."

The two Brawns stayed 1–2 through their first refuelling stops, but Jenson was worried that he might get boxed in behind Felipe Massa's fuel-heavy Ferrari as the race unfolded, unless Rubens got his skates on. In order to hedge their bets, at that first round of stops Brawn took the tactical decision to switch Jenson to a two-stop strategy, fuelling him up for another 29 laps. But Rubens still reckoned he could win on his established three-stop strategy. In the end, it was Jenson who won by a fraction over 13 seconds. Now he had 41 points to Barrichello's 27. But there was tension in the air. Rubens made it clear that he would hang up his helmet if there were any indication of strategic favouritism towards Jenson.

Button dismissed this, repeating that he felt he was being held up. "I was thinking only of Massa and Vettel," he explained. "We knew that Massa was heavy and the last thing I needed was to be stuck behind him after my pit stop. I wanted to open a gap. I wanted Rubens to pick up the pace."

In fact, anybody who thought Jenson was receiving special treatment only had to wait until the next race, that frantic scramble through the streets of Monte Carlo. Five years before, driving for BAR, Jenson had delivered there brilliantly, with a close second place to Jarno Trulli's Renault. However, during Thursday practice for the 2009 race, the Briton seemed as though he was making heavy weather of the epic street circuit, team-mate Barrichello finishing ahead of him in both sessions.

But when it mattered, Jenson pulled everything together brilliantly – a blend of total discipline, mechanical sympathy for the car and huge self-restraint. Pole was his. During the race, he used the softer of the two Bridgestone tyre compounds for his opening stint, his deft touch earning him a 13sec lead over Barrichello by the time he stopped to fit a set of the less delicate, harder, prime tyres

← ← **Jenson shadows team-mate Rubens Barrichello during the opening stages of the Spanish Grand Prix.**
📷 LAT

↑ **Leading the field through the narrow streets of Monaco.**
📷 LAT

← **Jenson runs down the startline straight towards the Royal Box at Monaco after mistakenly stopping his car in *parc fermé*.**
📷 LAT

↑**Six out of seven.
Jenson salutes his
delighted pit crew
as he takes a hard-
fought win ahead
of Sebastian
Vettel at the
Turkish Grand Prix.**
📷 LAT

after just 17 laps. By then the job was done and another
brilliant victory secured.

Yet having driven all that distance in exacting and
demanding circumstances, Jenson was still as fresh as
a new pin. Forgetting that the first three finishers at
Monaco are supposed to stop in front of the Royal Box on
the startline straight, Jenson pulled into the customary
parc fermé. He then had to run down the straight before
he could collect his trophy. Piece of cake!

There was more of the same coming at Istanbul Park,
home of the Turkish Grand Prix, and proof positive that
it is possible to build a highly demanding race track while
still taking into account contemporary safety constraints
in terms of run-off areas and suitable crash barriers.

Vettel was on pole by a whisker, with Jenson alongside
on the front row. The young Red Bull driver made a clean
start to lead as the pack got away from the grid, but on the
high-speed approach to the downhill turn nine, Vettel's Red
Bull was slightly unsettled by the effects of a cross-wind. It
was just enough to put him into a wobble, causing him to
run wide on the left. In the split-second he took to correct it,
Jenson was through into a lead he would never lose.

Fair enough, it was close. Red Bull switched Sebastian to
a three-stop strategy, which meant he was filling Button's
mirrors after each of the Brawn's refuelling stops. "We even
have great mirrors on this car," said the winner, "so I was able
to clock him whenever he jinked a little. It was a lot of fun…"

Button later summed up his Turkish delight by saying that

the Brawn "suited my style perfectly. It was outrageous. Just fantastic." He now led the World Championship by 26 points from Barrichello, and 32 points from third-placed Vettel. Difficult to imagine at the time, but this was to be the end of the easy bit of Jenson's challenge for the World Championship.

As for Rubens, he was getting tense and wound up about things. It was hard for him to conceal his frustration over the fact that Button kept beating him. During the Turkish Grand Prix weekend, he had a re-run of the glitch with his clutch and anti-stall mechanism which had slowed him off the line in Melbourne, was pitched into a spin as he diced with Lewis Hamilton's McLaren, and grappled with an apparent rev limiter problem which might have been exacerbated by a change of wind direction on race day. It was getting on his nerves.

Jenson was obviously hoping to be in a position to sustain momentum into the British Grand Prix weekend at Silverstone, for which crucial race the Brawn-Mercedes would be fitted with a significant aerodynamic upgrade. That was the intention, anyway, but after the team struggled in Friday free practice with low tyre temperatures, and consequently dire levels of grip, the new

↑ **Jenson sports a special helmet design for the British Grand Prix as he listens to a little advice from racing legend Sir Stirling Moss.**
📷 LAT

← **A difficult weekend at Silverstone saw Jenson qualify and finish sixth in his home race.**
📷 LAT

"MY LAST STINT [IN THE RACE] AT SILVERSTONE SHOWED THAT THE PACE OF THE CAR IS REALLY COMPETITIVE, SO WE'RE CONFIDENT WE CAN TURN IT ROUND FOR THIS RACE"

JENSON BUTTON

components were not fitted for Saturday qualifying. The team suddenly found itself in the unfortunate, indeed unfamiliar, position of trying to play catch-up.

It was a miserable race for Jenson. He qualified sixth and that's where he finished, on this occasion eclipsed by Rubens who came home third on one of his favourite circuits. Only when he switched to the softer of the two Bridgestone tyre compounds in the closing stages of the race could Button find any pace in his car, slashing into Nico Rosberg's fifth-place advantage, but unable to get past the Williams once he actually caught it up.

It was that spurt, on a day when Vettel and Webber delivered a profoundly worrying 1–2 for Red Bull, which convinced Jenson that he should keep calm. There were quantifiable reasons for the Brawn's lack of pace at Silverstone, so he arrived at Nürburgring for the German Grand Prix still feeling upbeat and confident.

"My last stint [in the race] at Silverstone showed that the pace of the car is really competitive, so we're confident we can turn it round for this race," he bubbled.

Ross Brawn added: "We have several new aerodynamic parts which were not used in qualifying [at Silverstone] due to the issues that we faced there [tyre temperatures], along with additional improvements scheduled for Nürburgring which should position us well going into the weekend."

Once again, the race weekend fell apart for the Brawn team, although they switched Jenson to a three-stop strategy which helped him squeeze a fifth place out of his run from third on the grid. Again, Brawn's weekend was stifled by low tyre temperatures and lack of grip. Barrichello followed Jenson across the line in sixth place, furious that he'd apparently been disadvantaged strategically by the team yet again.

This wasn't quite true, of course. The team was taking what it judged, in the heat of battle, to the best route by which to bring its cars home in the strongest possible finishing positions. At the end of the day, Rubens set only the 11th-fastest lap of the race, which was not really good enough. But Ross Brawn very charmingly paid tribute to Rubens's loyalty and said their good relationship would not be jeopardised by this brief outburst.

If Nürburgring was bad, Hungaroring was a disaster. In qualifying, Barrichello's Brawn lost a rear spring, which bounced down the road behind him before hitting Ferrari driver Felipe Massa on the helmet, leaving the Brazilian with serious head injuries from which, mercifully, he made a remarkable recovery.

Understandably, the FIA officials wanted to inspect the rear of Button's car for safety reasons. Fuelled up for two runs during the final qualifying session, Jenson had

← No prizes for guessing who these fans are rooting for at the British Grand Prix.
◎ LAT

→ A hive of activity as the crew attend to Jenson's car during a pit stop at the Hungarian Grand Prix.
◎ LAT

← Jenson took time out during the German Grand Prix weekend to give a few lucky passengers a ride around the Nürburgring circuit.
◎ LAT

to miss the first run and finished up 8th, on the fourth row. The upside was that he could run a long opening stint. But the low ambient temperatures and consequent lack of grip from the Brawn's tyres left him struggling home 7th in the race, complaining desperately over the radio link "Why, oh why is this car so difficult to drive?" If only there had been an easy answer.

Hungary had been a huge disappointment, somehow representing yet another symbolic counter-point to Jenson's success there three years earlier. Having taken six victories out of the first seven races, the Brawn team, which had seemed so technically assertive and on top of the job during that crucial opening phase of the year, was not only struggling, but the reasons as to just why the team had lost its edge seemed ever-more elusive to pinpoint and difficult to correct.

The simple facts of the matter were that the Brawn chassis did not seem to warm up its tyres to the levels required to generate competitive grip. At Silverstone and Nürburgring there was the apparently legitimate excuse that cool conditions prevailed, but in Hungary it was significantly warmer – although by no means as torrid as it has been at the circuit near Budapest in the past.

"I've lost an average of five points per race to [Mark] Webber in the last three races," pondered Jenson. "At that rate he will be ahead of me in four races's time, with three races left to go.

"The car was good in Friday practice. We had the best

tyre performance of all the cars, with plenty of grip and very low wear rates. Nothing changed on the car between Friday and the race. The only thing different was that the temperature on Friday was 10-degrees warmer."

Although in the four-week break between Budapest and Valencia the F1 community submitted itself to a technical lock-down – all the teams agreeing to close their design, development and manufacturing facilities as a structured programme to save money – no regulation has ever been written which would prevent any technical staff from 'thinking' about how to improve their cars during such a period of enforced inactivity.

So, during the break Jenson Button enjoyed a two-week holiday in the south of France with his girlfriend Jessica, as well as keeping his physical fitness at peak level with preparations to compete in a triathlon event. But he was soon back to the serious business of the season and hoping for better prospects for the European Grand Prix.

Certainly the weather in Valencia did not suggest that the Brawn-Mercedes would have any problems warming up its tyres to a decent operating temperature. When Jenson and Jessica arrived in the paddock on the Thursday afternoon prior to the race, there was hardly the slightest trace of a breeze blowing in across the waterfront marina to take the edge off the sweltering 30-degree temperature.

"We know, or rather we think we know, from the data where we went wrong," said Jenson cautiously. "You never know 100 per cent, for sure, until you get to the circuit and test it, but we think we understand the car and the issues that we have and hopefully they will be solved at this race."

After Saturday morning's free practice session, with qualifying beckoning in possibly the most sweltering temperatures since Bahrain, Ross Brawn was sounding very much more optimistic. "We are back to dealing with a normal car again rather than chasing tyre temperatures," he said with a cautious smile. But the race turned out to be a disappointment.

In the closing stages, Jenson managed to squeeze out of his Brawn the sort of speed and performance that Barrichello had demonstrated throughout the race. Clearly, the World Championship leader had swapped the uninhibited effervescence which had characterised the early part of his year for a more cautious and strategic approach. But by trying to drive tactically, he was also starting to drive tentatively.

Button could not blame the car when Barrichello made good use of his to score his first win of the season and become a serious threat. The Brawn drivers were still free to race each other, but their more immediate concern was positively to establish whether the car's return to form

was due to the hot weather needed to make the car work temperature into its tyres.

"This was the first time when we have had a strong car that I have not been able to get the most out of it," said Button. "That is the most frustrating thing. We have to turn that around. The Red Bulls are still going to be fighting, they are going to be quick for sure over the next few races, especially the next one at Spa.

"I think we have sorted out a few of our issues, and we have some updates. The team has proven that we are quick when it is hot, and Spa will be the tell-tale of whether we are quick when it is cold. There are a few coolish races still to come. So this Friday [when practice for the Belgian Grand Prix would begin], is a very important day for us to see if we have made improvements in the cool conditions."

Button arrived at Spa determined to press on hard. The media had been dropping hints to the effect that Jenson was feeling the pressure, that he'd had it all a bit too easy early on in what had been very much a 'front-loaded' season from the viewpoint of racing victories. In response, Jenson just kept his own counsel.

"I don't have a conservative approach, that's the thing," he mused. "If you look at the last four races, the first three of those four, our car was not as competitive as we would have hoped when I was winning races.

"So if you get rid of them, and then look at the last one (Valencia), it wasn't a good race weekend for me, initially because I didn't qualify well. Then, if you'd looked at the race, if I'd stayed on the circuit on the inside of Vettel (on the opening lap) I would have broken my front wing and wiped him out as well."

Yet, for all his optimism, Jenson continued to be bogged down in this unexpected performance rut throughout practice and qualifying for the Belgian Grand Prix. Again, he was eclipsed by Barrichello, who lined up third. Button could only manage 14th.

"I THINK WE HAVE SORTED OUT A FEW OF OUR ISSUES, AND WE HAVE SOME UPDATES. THE TEAM HAS PROVEN THAT WE ARE QUICK WHEN IT IS HOT"

JENSON BUTTON

↑ **We are not amused!
Jenson, Romain Grosjean
and Lewis Hamilton look
mean and moody after
ending their race on the
first lap at Spa.**
📷 LAT

↓ **An expensive second-hand car lot at the
Belgian Grand Prix. Jenson's stricken
Brawn lies with Lewis Hamilton's McLaren,
Jaime Alguersuari's Toro Rosso and
Romain Grosjean's Renault, after a series
of incidents on the chaotic first lap.**
📷 LAT

"I think Jenson is showing all the classic signs of a
driver who is trying too hard," said retired triple World
Champion Niki Lauda. "You have a good start to your
season, win a lot of races, and then suddenly you find
things going wrong. In order to respond to the situation
you try to drive tactically and begin making mistakes. It's
been quite a common pattern over the years.

"But the really worrying thing is that Brawn continue
to talk about problems with tyre temperatures, but their
other guy is up at the front, which must add to Jenson's
worry and feeling of nervousness."

Come the Belgian race, Button had precious little
opportunity to make amends to his critics. At the end
of the long 205mph straight beyond Eau Rouge, braking
hard for the tight ess-bend that followed, Jenson
was tapped into a spin by Renault new-boy Romain
Grosjean. He ended up against the barriers, along with his
compatriot Lewis Hamilton's McLaren. He had the long
walk back to the pits during which to contemplate the
stark reality that he had failed to finish a race for the first
time during the 2010 season.

When he arrived at the pits, he had to sit and watch as

> ## "IT WAS A MUCH-NEEDED MOVE, AS WITHOUT IT I WOULD HAVE PROBABLY FINISHED THIRD OR FOURTH"
>
> **JENSON BUTTON**

Barrichello, who had a slow getaway from the grid, came home 7th, his Brawn surviving a spell in the closing stages of the race trailing a plume of oil smoke from its leaking gearbox. Button now had 72 points, Barrichello 56. Now Monza, that flat-out blast through the former royal park on the outskirts of Milan, one of the great monuments to the sport's historic traditions, lay ahead to round off the frenetic schedule which had made up the European leg of the season.

Thankfully, the Brawns were now back on the pace, Rubens and Jenson qualifying fifth and sixth, both with heavy fuel loads which allowed them to make the most out of one-stop race strategies. And Jenson was up to the job when it came to first-lap audacity. Rubens nipped ahead of Heikki Kovalainen's McLaren-Mercedes, fourth on the starting grid, as they went away from the line, and Jenson knew he would have to follow him through quickly if his Brazilian colleague was not to make a decisive break early on.

Going into the second Lesmo right-hander, a really tricky high-speed turn if entered on a tight line, Jenson forced his way inside Kovalainen and hung on to the advantage. "It was a much-needed move, as without it I would have probably finished third or fourth," he acknowledged.

Lewis Hamilton's McLaren initially led from pole, but the World Champion was on a two-stop strategy, and when he came in for fuel for the first time on lap 15, he lost the lead to Kimi Räikkönen's Ferrari. The Finn made his first stop on lap 19, allowing Rubens to surge through to lead by 2.4sec from Jenson. The one-stop strategy would be totally vindicated, and Barrichello eventually crossed the finishing line 2.8sec ahead of his friend and colleague, Räikkönen taking a third-place consolation prize for Ferrari after Hamilton crashed spectacularly, but thankfully without injury, on the final lap.

With Red Bull having another bad day, the World

⬆ **Pushing hard to keep the pressure on team-mate and winner Barrichello during the Italian Grand Prix, as the pendulum swung back in favour of Brawn GP.**
📷 sutton-images.com

⬇ **Friends and rivals. Jenson and Rubens congratulate each other after another 1–2 for Brawn in the Italian Grand Prix at Monza.**
📷 LAT

Under the spotlights on the streets of Marina Bay in Singapore. Jenson drove a storming race from 12th on the grid to finish fifth.
LAT

Hotly pursued by Robert Kubica's BMW-Sauber and Fernando Alonso's Renault, Jenson shadows Rubens Barrichello during the Japanese Grand Prix at Suzuka.
LAT

Championship contest was suddenly coalescing into a two-horse race between the Brawn team-mates, with Rubens making a late charge for the title. Yet, for all their rivalry, there was no concealing the genuine affection and regard existing between the two men as they joshed and hugged each other prior to going out onto the Monza rostrum.

Jenson now led the championship on 80 points, with Rubens now 14 points behind on 66. But Sebastian Vettel had now dropped back, with 54 points, and although there were still 40 points to race for over the remaining four races, the momentum was now very much with the Brawn duo.

"Concentrating on one person for sure has to be a little bit easier," said Jenson. "I've got to stay as close as possible to Rubens, but I still want to win races. I know I am in a very good situation at the moment. I'm driving the best car on the grid at the moment and I've probably got one of the most competitive team-mates on the grid at the moment. So there are lots of positives and a couple of negatives there, but why shouldn't I be positive?"

A fortnight later, Lewis Hamilton demonstrated the McLaren team's renewed potency with a crushing victory in the second Singapore Grand Prix, held under floodlights at the spectacular Marina Bay circuit. The 24-year-old British driver was never seriously challenged on a day when all his key rivals were either spinning, colliding, grazing the wall, or simply not driving very quickly behind him.

Jenson finished fifth, just ahead of Barrichello, to stretch his championship lead by another point to 15 with three races to go. By running further than Rubens on his second stint, with a heavier fuel load, Button vaulted ahead of the Brazilian at his last refuelling stop, after which both drivers were told to ease back to conserve their brakes, which suffer a real hammering on this tortuous circuit.

Button did so, driving with one eye on his mirror, but Barrichello kept his foot down and almost caught Jenson on the line. It was some while before they exchanged pleasantries after the race, but that's what you expect from two team-mates who are battling each other for the World Championship.

Button was delighted. "I came away with a result which doesn't look so good on paper, but it's almost like a victory to win these points," he said. "Psychologically, you will have to ask Rubens. Factually, it means that I have won more points. I have a 15-point lead instead of 14 points.

"Rubens can still beat me, for sure, but this result has taken a lot of weight off my shoulders, so it is a good finish." Even one or two Brawn team insiders smiled indulgently when someone remarked that Jenson and Rubens seemed as though they were locked in a three-legged race for the title crown, neither quite able to make a decisive break. It was a whole lot more complicated than that, of course.

Yet, in truth, the outcome of the title chase remained very finely balanced indeed. Unquestionably, Barrichello, buoyed by those victories at Valencia and Monza, was catching his second wind. The Brazilian's slightly tentative and nervous demeanour, so apparent during those early months of the season when Button was rattling away the wins almost on a fortnightly basis, had given way to a steely confidence not obviously apparent since his great days as Michael Schumacher's wing man at Ferrari.

Jackie Stewart, for one, was certainly impressed, and appreciated that Jenson needed to take strong account of the Brazilian's counter-attack. It was not a development which totally surprised the Scottish triple champion.

"Technically, from the point of view of setting up the car, Rubens, I would argue, is the best driver on the grid," said Stewart. "That was an important factor in Brawn retaining him for this season. (But) since Turkey there has been, for whatever reason, a silence from Button, a lack of delivery.

"His team-mate has won twice and generally outperformed him in the second half of the season. That, rightly or wrongly, affects how people see him."

Button went into the Japanese GP at Suzuka with his confidence under tight rein. But it was confidence nonetheless.

"It sounds silly, but it is a bit of a rollercoaster when you're fighting for a championship, and it's been a long time since I've been fighting for a championship, so you do forget," he said. "But if it was easy we'd all be doing it.

A winning smile. Jessica Michibata shows support for her man during the Japanese Grand Prix weekend.
LAT

↑ After a disastrous wet second qualifying session at Interlagos, Jenson lined up 14th on the grid for the Brazilian Grand Prix, having failed to make it through to the final session.
📷 sutton-images.com

It's part of the challenge, it's a sport that is very emotional for me. I've always loved motor racing since I was very, very young, and being in the position that I'm in, I'm certainly very privileged and very lucky to be fighting for a championship, so I will never forget that. And I also have some great people around me who keep me grounded and focused. It's obviously tough, but it's also very exciting and I wouldn't change it for the world, for sure."

Japan was frustrating for another reason. Sebastian Vettel, who had remained a credible but outside contender for the title, reasserted his challenge with a dramatic and dominant victory at Suzuka. He qualified his Red Bull on pole position and dominated the race from the start. Jenson finished eighth, this time one place behind Rubens.

So the additional one-point advantage Jenson had achieved in Singapore the previous week had been wiped out at a stroke.

Advice directed towards Jenson was coming thick and fast from third parties. This blizzard of well-intentioned comment was welcome and frustrating in pretty much equal measure but, like Stewart, Damon Hill had some valuable observations.

In Damon's view, Jenson should ignore all strategic advice on how to clinch the World Championship and just continue concentrating on doing it his way over the two remaining races on the 2009 schedule.

"Everyone is looking for him (Button) to clinch the championship as quickly and decisively as possible," said Hill. "But it is his career, his championship campaign and it may be nerve-wracking to watch for those of us who are supporting him, but he's the one facing the challenge, he's the one doing the job.

"In situations like this you just have to do what you think is best at the time. There's no point in worrying what anybody else is doing, because the only performance he can influence is his own. It was a similar situation when Jacques and I were contesting the championship. I knew I had done the best job I could preparing for the final race of the season, after which I just had to get on with it and see how events unfolded.

"WE KEEP GETTING OURSELVES INTO THESE TRICKY QUALIFYING SITUATIONS AND WE ARE THEN GETTING OURSELVES OUT OF THEM IN THE RACE"

JENSON BUTTON

"Ultimately you can only do what your car is capable of. There were a few moments in '96 when I thought I might be able to close the job down before the end of the season, but these opportunities are not always as straightforward as they seem."

Hill added: "I wish Jenson well. I think it would be really terrific for the sport in this country if we had back-to-back World Champions, Jenson following on from Lewis (Hamilton). But he must do it his way."

For his part, Button believed that the momentum was with him, even though he had to battle through from 12th place on the starting grid at Suzuka, following a grid penalty which made it even harder work to come through to an eventual eighth.

"We are doing the best job we can in a difficult situation," he said of the Brawn team, "(But) we keep getting ourselves into these tricky (qualifying) situations and we are then getting ourselves out of them in the race."

Now there were only two races remaining, each taking place on a circuit which could hardly be more diametrically opposed to the other. The penultimate round of the title chase was scheduled for Sao Paulo's wild and woolly Interlagos track, where Emerson Fittipaldi had first put Brazilian motor racing on the map in 1973 with a victory for Lotus in the country's first ever World Championship qualifying round.

Two weeks later, the season would come to an end at a mega-million-dollar track at Abu Dhabi in the United Arab Emirates. The organisers of this dramatic and spectacular new circuit were hoping against hope that the championship contest would go right down to the wire. You could understand their viewpoint. But as far as Jenson was concerned, he preferred the idea of getting the whole thing done and dusted in Brazil.

Yet, suddenly it looked as though Rubens Barrichello might, just might, turn the whole season upside-down. He badly wanted to win the Brazilian Grand Prix and join Fittipaldi, Nelson Piquet, Ayrton Senna and Felipe Massa in that exclusive pantheon of national heroes who'd won either here or in Rio. Rubens, remember, grew up in the family home barely a stone's throw from the Interlagos paddock. For the 37-year-old Brazilian, that elusive home victory would mean more, much more, than simply another step up the ladder which might conceivably carry him to the World Championship.

In F1 terms, there is rain, there is a deluge – and there is a Brazilian storm at Interlagos. Such a downpour assailed qualifying at the Brazilian track, and while Barrichello surfed his way through to grab pole position, Jenson missed the top-ten cut and had to be satisfied with 14th. It was a qualifying position fraught with potential hazards, not least

→ At the start of a mercurial drive in the Brazilian Grand Prix, Jenson battles with Romain Grosjean. He would pass the Renault driver with a brave move around the outside on lap 6.
📷 LAT

→ Another lap, another pass. Jenson dives inside Kazuki Nakajima's Williams on lap 7, latching on to the rear wing of Grand Prix debutant Kamui Kobayashi's Toyota.
📷 LAT

→ After a long and frustrating battle lasting some 18 laps, Jenson finally makes a move stick on the feisty Kobayashi on lap 25. This freed him to run in clear air, allowing him to up his pace.
📷 LAT

→ Shortly after his first pit stop, Jenson makes another bold outbraking move, this time on Sebastien Buemi's Toro Rosso for seventh place. The title was now within sight.
📷 sutton-images.com

→ **A dream fulfilled. Jenson and John Button celebrate the culmination of all their efforts and sacrifices along the path to the world title.**

sutton-images.com

↓ **"I'm World Champion!" – the expression says it all.**

sutton-images.com

the psychological pressure of the capacity crowd chanting "Rubinho, Rubinho!" almost as one from the moment Jenson's Brawn pulled up on its allotted starting position on the seventh row of the grid.

Yet, when the starting lights went out, Jenson came alive. The Englishman dodged this way and that through the frenetic first-lap traffic jam which claimed three of his rivals. By the end of the opening lap he was up to ninth, then the safety car was deployed to slow the field while the debris of a collision between Jarno Trulli's Toyota and Adrian Sutil's Force India was cleared up.

When the field was unleashed again, Button went back to work as a man inspired. Decisively, he dispatched the Renault of Romain Grosjean, then the Williams of Kazuki Nakajima. His next target in the high-speed queue was Toyota new boy Kamui Kobayashi, who was guesting for the injured Timo Glock. Kobayashi held out for 18 laps before succumbing to an inspired Button pass, then it was the turn of Toro Rosso's Sébastien Buemi to get elbowed aside.

After Barrichello dropped back with a puncture, Jenson's crucial fifth place was secure, the finishing position he needed to ensure that he succeeded Lewis Hamilton as

"I'M WORLD CHAMPION, BABY!"
JENSON BUTTON

← The spectacular new Yas Marina circuit in Abu Dhabi provided a stunning setting for the final race of the 2009 season. Here, Jenson powers past the Yas Hotel, through which the track runs.
📷 LAT

the next British World Champion. In the back of the Brawn garage John Button and Jenson's manager Richard Goddard could hardly bear to watch.

"For the last seven or eight laps we were all crying like little girls," said 'Old Boy', fighting back the tears.

Suddenly it was all over. Jenson shaved the pit wall singing "We are the Champions" as he stormed past the chequered flag. The job was done. "I'm World Champion, baby," he screamed. "That race deserved it." It did indeed.

The remarkable billion-dollar Yas Marina circuit, with its gigantic futuristic hotel actually straddling the track, was the final stopping-off point for the 2009 World Championship in Abu Dhabi. The second F1 race to be held in the Gulf region, after Bahrain, it really was the most remarkable facility and while both Jenson and Rubens felt from the outset that the track layout would play to the strengths of their Brawn-Mercedes, it was frustrating for Jenson to line up only fifth on the grid.

Lewis Hamilton took an easy pole in the McLaren-Mercedes, leading the race ahead of Sebastian Vettel's Red Bull, before the 2008 World Champion was called into the pits and withdrawn from the race on safety grounds, after his car developed a suspected problem with its right-rear brake.

This left Vettel to cruise to an easy victory, with Jenson simply storming up onto the tail of Mark Webber in the closing stages, but ultimately unable to prevent the gritty Australian from rounding off another Red Bull 1–2.

"After the second stop I found I had very good grip with the (softer) option tyre," enthused Jenson. "I had very good initial turn-in, which meant I could carry a lot of speed through (the corners). That's why I was able to close down Mark.

"The last couple of laps were a lot of fun. I couldn't make the move stick. I was very excited by the battle, and I thought I could pull it off, but Mark is always a very difficult person to overtake. We were clean but on the edge, so it was perfect. Disappointed not to get that second place, but I really enjoyed the fight today, and today for me has been a bonus after winning the championship in Brazil."

↓ Jenson ended the 2009 season on a high in Abu Dhabi, battling on the limit with Mark Webber for second place during the closing laps. Jenson finished third, behind the two Red Bull drivers.
📷 sutton-images.com

CAREER STATISTICS

1990
British Cadet karting champion.

1991
British Cadet karting champion winning all 34 races.
He also won the British Open Kart Championship.

1992
Won British Open Kart Championship and British Junior TKM titles.

1993
Won British Open Kart Championship for third time.

1994
Fourth in British Junior TKM Kart Championship.

1995
Won Senior ICA Italian Kart Championship. He was the youngest ever runner-up in the Formula A world championship.

1996
Third in both World Cup and American Kart Series.

1997
Won European Supercup A Kart Championship driving for Team GKS Tecno Rotax Bridgestone. Winner of Ayrton Senna Memorial Cup at Suzuka.

1998
Formula Ford
Won TOCA Slick 50 British Championship driving a Mygale for Haywood Racing with nine race wins. Winner Brands Hatch Formula Ford Festival. Runner-up in European FF Championship.

1999
British Formula 3 Championship
Third – three wins (Team Promatecme)

Formula 1 Tests
- Prost-Peugeot AP02
- McLaren-Mercedes MP4/13
- Williams-BMW FW21B

FORMULA 1

2000

8th in championship (Williams-BMW) 12 points

ROUND	VENUE	GRID	RACE	FASTEST LAP
1	Australia	21st	DNF (engine)	10th
2	Brazil	9th	6th	8th
3	San Marino	18th	DNF (engine)	22nd
4	Britain	6th	5th	7th
5	Spain	10th	17th	4th
6	Europe (Nürburgring)	11th	10th	10th
7	Monaco	14th	DNF (oil pressure)	21st
8	Canada	18th	11th	16th
9	France	10th	8th	11th
10	Austria	18th	5th	8th
11	Germany (Hockenheim)	16th	4th	11th
12	Hungary	8th	9th	9th
13	Belgium	3rd	5th	8th
14	Italy	12th	DNF (crash)	15th
15	USA	6th	DNF (engine)	21st
16	Japan	5th	5th	5th
17	Malaysia	16th	DNF (engine)	17th

2001

17th in championship (Benetton-Renault) 2 points

ROUND	VENUE	GRID	RACE	FASTEST LAP
1	Australia	16th	14th	15th
2	Malaysia	17th	11th	14th
3	Brazil	20th	10th	20th
4	San Marino	21st	12th	18th
5	Spain	21st	15th	18th
6	Austria	21st	DNF (engine)	13th
7	Monaco	17th	7th	10th
8	Canada	20th	DNF (oil leak)	17th
9	Europe (Nürburgring)	20th	13th	14th
10	France	17th	16th	16th
11	Britain	18th	15th	16th
12	Germany (Hockenheim)	18th	5th	11th
13	Hungary	17th	DNF (spin)	14th
14	Belgium	10th	DNF (crash)	11th
15	Italy	11th	DNF (engine)	18th
16	USA	10th	9th	10th
17	Japan	9th	7th	9th

2002

7th in championship (Renault) 14 points

ROUND	VENUE	GRID	RACE	FASTEST LAP
1	Australia	11th	DNF (crash)	No time
2	Malaysia	8th	4th	7th
3	Brazil	7th	4th	4th
4	San Marino	9th	5th	7th
5	Spain	6th	12th	8th
6	Austria	13th	7th	7th
7	Monaco	8th	DNF (crash)	13th
8	Canada	13th	15th	14th
9	Europe (Nürburgring)	8th	5th	4th
10	Britain	12th	12th	14th
11	France	7th	6th	6th
12	Germany (Hockenheim)	13th	DNF (transmission)	19th
13	Hungary	9th	DNF (spin)	16th
14	Belgium	10th	DNF (engine)	17th
15	Italy	17th	5th	12th
16	USA	14th	8th	12th
17	Japan	10th	6th	9th

2003

9th equal in championship (BAR-Honda) 17 points

ROUND	VENUE	GRID	RACE	FASTEST LAP
1	Australia	8th	10th	7th
2	Malaysia	9th	7th	11th
3	Brazil	11th	DNF (crash)	13th
4	San Marino	9th	8th	8th
5	Spain	5th	9th	7th
6	Austria	7th	4th	7th
7	Monaco	20th	DNS	No time
8	Canada	17th	DNF (gearbox)	9th
9	Europe (Nürburgring)	12th	7th	11th
10	France	14th	DNF (out of fuel)	10th
11	Britain	20th	8th	14th
12	Germany (Hockenheim)	17th	8th	8th
13	Hungary	14th	10th	9th
14	Italy	7th	DNF (gearbox)	8th
15	USA	11th	DNF (hydraulics)	8th
16	Japan	9th	4th	6th

2004

3rd in championship (BAR-Honda) 85 points

ROUND	VENUE	GRID	RACE	FASTEST LAP
1	Australia	4th	6th	7th
2	Malaysia	6th	3rd	3rd
3	Bahrain	6th	3rd	5th
4	San Marino	1st	2nd	2nd
5	Spain	14th	8th	2nd
6	Monaco	2nd	2nd	3rd
7	Europe (Nürburgring)	5th	3rd	4th
8	Canada	2nd	3rd	5th
9	USA	4th	DNF (gearbox)	5th
10	France	4th	5th	5th
11	Britain	3rd	4th	3rd
12	Germany (Hockenheim)	13th	2nd	2nd
13	Hungary	4th	5th	4th
14	Belgium	12th	DNF (puncture)	12th
15	Italy	6th	3rd	6th
16	China	3rd	2nd	4th
17	Japan	5th	3rd	6th
18	Brazil	5th	DNF (engine)	20th

2005

9th in championship (BAR-Honda) 37 points

ROUND	VENUE	GRID	RACE	FASTEST LAP
1	Australia	8th	11th	4th
2	Malaysia	9th	DNF (oil leak)	14th
3	Bahrain	11th	DNF (clutch)	5th
4	San Marino	3rd	DISQUALIFIED	2nd
5	Spain	EXCLUDED FROM COMPETING		
6	Monaco	EXCLUDED FROM COMPETING		
7	Europe (Nürburgring)	13th	10th	11th
8	Canada	1st	DNF (accident)	6th
9	USA	3rd	WITHDREW	
10	France	7th	4th	4th
11	Britain	2nd	5th	7th
12	Germany (Hockenheim)	2nd	3rd	3rd
13	Hungary	8th	5th	6th
14	Turkey	13th	5th	5th
15	Italy	3rd	8th	9th
16	Belgium	8th	3rd	5th
17	Brazil	4th	7th	10th
18	Japan	2nd	5th	5th
19	China	4th	8th	12th

2006

6th in championship (Honda) 56 points

ROUND	VENUE	GRID	RACE	FASTEST LAP
1	Bahrain	3rd	4th	5th
2	Malaysia	2nd	3rd	4th
3	Australia	1st	DNF (engine)	7th
4	San Marino	2nd	7th	7th
5	Europe (Nürburgring)	6th	DNF (engine)	13th
6	Spain	8th	6th	6th
7	Monaco	13th	11th	8th
8	Britain	19th	DNF (oil leak)	17th
9	Canada	8th	9th	13th
10	USA	7th	DNF (damage)	13th
11	France	17th	DNF (engine)	11th
12	Germany (Hockenheim)	4th	4th	7th
13	Hungary	14th	1st	3rd
14	Turkey	6th	4th	4th
15	Italy	5th	5th	7th
16	China	4th	4th	5th
17	Japan	7th	4th	5th
18	Brazil	14th	3rd	4th

2007
14th equal in championship (Honda) 6 points

ROUND	VENUE	GRID	RACE	FASTEST LAP
1	Australia	14th	15th	17th
2	Malaysia	15th	12th	16th
3	Bahrain	16th	DNF (accident)	none recorded
4	Spain	14th	12th	13th
5	Monaco	10th	11th	9th
6	Canada	15th	DNF (gears)	none recorded
7	USA	13th	12th	14th
8	France	12th	8th	7th
9	Britain	18th	10th	17th
10	Europe (Nürburgring)	17th	DNF (accident)	21st
11	Hungary	17th	DNF (sensor)	21st
12	Turkey	21st	13th	10th
13	Italy	10th	8th	9th
14	Belgium	12th	DNF (hydraulics)	16th
15	Japan	6th	DNF (accident)	19th
16	China	10th	5th	6th
17	Brazil	16th	DNF (engine)	11th

2008
18th in championship (Honda) 3 points

ROUND	VENUE	GRID	RACE	FASTEST LAP
1	Australia	12th	DNF (accident)	none recorded
2	Malaysia	11th	10th	4th
3	Bahrain	9th	DNF (accident)	21st
4	Spain	13th	6th	5th
5	Turkey	13th	11th	13th
6	Monaco	11th	11th	10th
7	Canada	20th	11th	19th
8	France	16th	DNF (accident)	20th
9	Britain	17th	DNF (spin)	10th
10	Germany (Hockenheim)	14th	17th	16th
11	Hungary	12th	12th	14th
12	Europe (Valencia)	16th	13th	17th
13	Belgium	17th	15th	17th
14	Italy	19th	15th	4th
15	Singapore	12th	9th	15th
16	Japan	18th	14th	16th
17	China	18th	16th	14th
18	Brazil	17th	13th	10th

2009
1st in championship (Brawn) 95 points

ROUND	VENUE	GRID	RACE	FASTEST LAP
1	Australia	1st	1st	3rd
2	Malaysia	1st	1st	1st
3	China	5th	3rd	7th
4	Bahrain	4th	1st	3rd
5	Spain	1st	1st	2nd
6	Monaco	1st	1st	2nd
7	Turkey	2nd	1st	1st
8	Britain	6th	6th	4th
9	Germany (Nürburgring)	3rd	5th	6th
10	Hungary	8th	7th	6th
11	Europe (Valencia)	5th	7th	2nd
12	Belgium	14th	DNF (accident)	none recorded
13	Italy	6th	2nd	4th
14	Singapore	12th	5th	4th
15	Japan	7th	8th	5th
16	Brazil	14th	5th	7th
17	Abu Dhabi	5th	3rd	6th